SNEA KER

OBSE SSION

SNEA KER

OBSE SSION

Flammarion

CONTENTS

What Is a

Is a

The term "sneaker" comes from the verb "sneak." The word's invention is attributed to the author F. W. Robinson, in 1862, and to the American advertising executive Henry Nelson McKinney, in 1917. Both men used it to evoke the shoe's capacity to allow the wearer to move around silently, thanks to the rubber soles, as opposed to the noisier leather shoe that was the norm at the time.

Snea

A sneaker, also known as a trainer or runner, is a type of shoe that was originally designed for playing sports. The top part of the shoe, called the upper, can be made from different materials, but the shoe is typically lined with a rubber sole. Originally, cotton canvas was the most widely used material for the upper, but it has since been superseded by harder-wearing leather and its variants—suede, nubuck, etc. Velvet, jersey, synthetics, and recycled or bio-sourced materials are also often used.

Sneakers can be low top or high top (when the collar covers part or all of the ankle), with round or elongated toes, and soles of varying thickness. These forms, as well as the materials, were originally chosen and developed to support athletic performance. Now they are also selected for purely aesthetic reasons.

Anatomy
of a Sneaker

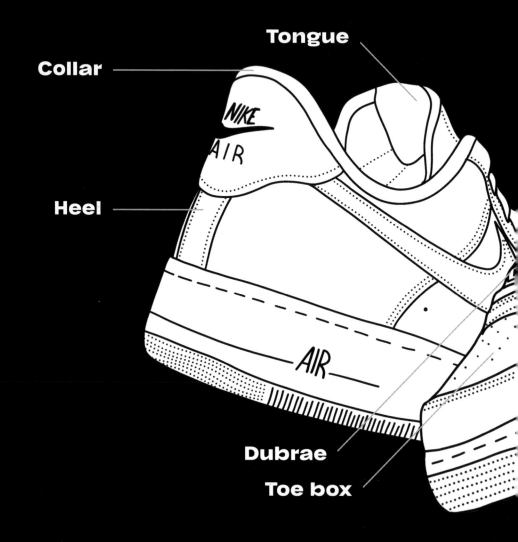

Tongue

Collar

Heel

Dubrae

Toe box

y

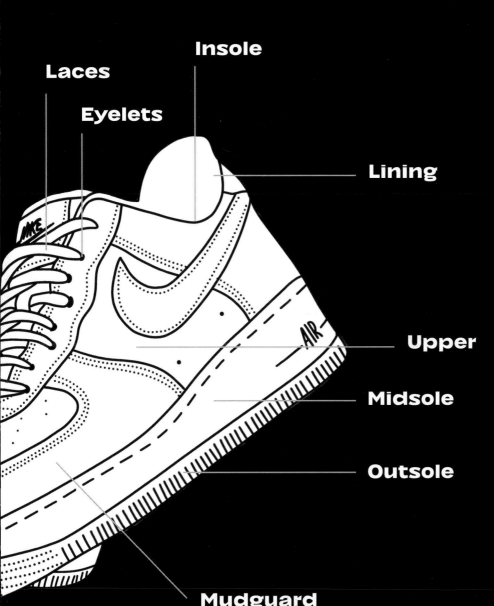

Insole

Laces

Eyelets

Lining

Upper

Midsole

Outsole

Mudguard

Snea Termin

The sneakerverse has its own vocabulary, rich with slang and abbreviations. These are the need-to-know terms.

BNIB
Stands for "brand new in box." Refers to unworn sneakers sold in their original box with all tags and accessories.

Bred
An abbreviation of "black and red." Although it originated with the Nike Air Jordan line, the term has come to refer to any black-and-red sneaker.

Campout
When fans wait outside a store overnight, sometimes for days, for a new sneaker release.

Cop
To buy a pair of sneakers.

CW
Stands for "colorway," the sneaker's box-listed colors.

Drop
The opposite of cop, i.e., not to buy a pair. Also refers more generally to a product release.

DS
Stands for "deadstock." Originally, the term referred to sneakers that were no longer sold by retailers and were only available on the resale market. However, it has come to mean a pair that has never been tried

kerology

F&F
Stands for "friends & family," a rare sneaker gifted only to friends and family of the brand's employees, or those of its partner.

Fufu
A slang term for "fake," used to designate a counterfeit sneaker.

GR
Stands for "general release" and usually refers to sneakers that are widely available to the public, as opposed to limited-edition releases.

Grail (or holy grail)
A sneaker grail is a rare model that is extremely hard to obtain. It can also be used to describe a sneakerhead's most desired, dream shoe. A holy grail is a pair that is almost impossible to cop.

L
Abbreviation of "lose" or "loss." To "take an L" means to lose out on a raffle.

Legit check
A legit check is done to verify a sneaker's authenticity.

OG
Initially stood for "Original Gangster," but has come to mean "original." Refers to the earliest release of a design, a classic colorway, or a faithful reissue.

Raffle
An online lottery for the opportunity to purchase a pair of sneakers—a marketing method frequently used by manufacturers and distributors.

Reseller
A person who buys sneakers to sell them on for a profit.

Restock
When a new batch of a previously sold-out sneaker is made and delivered to stores.

Sample
A prototype, created for testing or promotion, that is never mass-produced.

Sneakerhead
A person who collects sneakers as a hobby.

W
Abbreviation of "win," the opposite of "L." Refers to a winning raffle ticket.

The
Snea
Epic

ker's History

Sneakers have come a long way. Developed in the late nineteenth century, for decades they were simply sports equipment. They became symbols of style and objects of desire after an eventful history—one full of societal changes, technical advances, technological innovations, and cultural revolutions.

In the Beginning
There Was

Insuring Comfort in Summer Footwear
Shoes for outing, tennis and everyday use

ALL over the country men are wearing Keds this season. You will find them in town or at the seashore—on the street or at the tennis court—wherever you go for work or play.

Keds are the ideal footwear for warm weather. Their elastic rubber soles put new life in your step. Their soft, pliable fabric makes them always cool and comfortable.

Keds now include models made with regular welt soles and firmly boxed toes—just like leather shoes. This means a shoe of style and distinction—the very shoe you have needed to wear with your white flannels or Palm Beach suit.

With these additions, Keds are now a *complete line* of canvas summer shoes—ranging from the easy, less formal tennis shoe to the latest and most fashionable styles of footwear. Last year millions of pairs of Keds were worn by men, women and children.

Good dealers everywhere carry Keds. Ask to see the various models—notice how wonderfully light and comfortable they are. Look for the name Keds on the sole.

For men and women, $1.50—$6.00
For children . . . 1.15— 4.50

The standard shoes for tennis, boating and vacation wear. Made of light canvas, in high or low models—white or brown—with black, grey or red rubber soles.

Keds

One of the smart special types for summer wear. Made of the finest white canvas in high or Oxford models, with welt sole construction, which gives it all the style of leather shoes.

Sturdy shoes for sport and everyday wear — for boys and grownups—with or without heels. Made of heavy white or brown duck. Brown leather trimmings with ankle patch—red rubber soles and toe cap.

United States Rubber Company

Born of a revolutionary invention, sneakers were initially used exclusively for sports, and for decades many designers confined them to this specific role.

The history of the sneaker begins in 1839, with the invention of rubber vulcanization. The process, developed by Charles Goodyear, made it possible to produce the kind of soles we are familiar with today, and by the end of the century it was being used by the first athletic shoe manufacturers. The first sneakers were produced during a time when the world of sport was undergoing a radical change. With the first Olympic Games held in 1896, sports were being structured into clubs and federations, and the practice of physical exercise was strongly encouraged by public authorities—although the focus was more on preparedness for war than on personal well-being.

Left
A 1920s ad for Keds. Founded in 1916, the brand was a subsidiary of the United States Rubber Company, now Uniroyal.

Facing page
A Nike ad featuring the American tennis icon Billie Jean King, 1982.

Sport

A fledgling sports shoe industry took off in the early twentieth century: from leather cleats intended for track and field or football, to canvas basketball shoes made by the first large US manufacturers Keds and Converse. They garnered more fans after World War I, when societal advances like shorter workweeks or paid vacation allowed more people to indulge in leisure activities—and sneakers were their footwear of choice. Although social progress slowed during World War II, it resumed with renewed intensity during the postwar boom.

LONG MAY SHE REIGN

New manufacturers such as Adidas, Puma, and Asics appeared on the scene, leading to fierce competition to offer the best-performing shoes in each sport and to sponsor the best athletes. This was especially true for major events like the Olympics and the soccer World Cup, which increased in popularity with the first televised broadcasts. Nike joined the lineup of major sporting goods suppliers in the 1970s, a pivotal moment in the industry. Well-being was now a widespread concept, and running experienced its first boom, followed by fitness and basketball.

As new practices gained in popularity, the race to make the ideal shoe resumed with greater intensity. Product lines multiplied, and brands began outsourcing production to Asia, creating innovation hubs to design sneakers featuring the latest technology, like the Nike Air, Adidas Torsion, Asics Gel, and Reebok Pump. The quest for innovation persisted, and manufacturers made it their focus until the 1990s, remaining curiously averse to the idea of seeing their creations used off the playing field. But everything comes to those who wait—and sneakers were no exception.

Facing page
The 1975 Swiss women's
soccer championship final.

Right
An aerobics class in the
United States in the 1980s.

Below
The 100-meter final at the
1936 Summer Olympics in
Berlin, won by US athlete
Jesse Owens (in the
foreground).

Guess What ? "We're sorry, but we're working with sportswear, not fashion." This was Nike's response to the proposed collaboration with fashion designer Yohji Yamamoto, in 2002. Proof, if any were needed, that manufacturers have often focused solely on performance, to the exclusion of other qualities. The very first partnership with a non-athlete was only signed in 1986, with New York rap group Run-DMC.

Beyond the Sports

They may have been designed to enhance athletic performance—and were long confined to this role by their creators—but sneakers hit the streets early on, worn by youth subcultures as an anti-establishment symbol.

With each new social and technical advance, sneakers were repurposed and took on cultural significance. This journey from sportswear to statement accessory began after World War II: in the late 1940s, members of the Zazou movement in France danced to the frenetic rhythm of bebop jazz in canvas sneakers, a foreshadowing of the shoes' widespread appropriation by youth cultures.

Over the following decade, dress codes relaxed. The clothing worn by students at prestigious American universities—the Ivy League look—was the genesis of this casual style. US college students adopted a more relaxed look by keeping their sneakers on after gym class and throwing their blazers over their shoulders. Sneakers became a symbol of rebellion, a rejection of society's codes. And their first tottering steps soon extended far beyond American campuses.

The 1950s saw the rise of film and television, which helped spread popular culture. Stars of the silver screen such as James Dean, Marlon Brando, and Marilyn Monroe began to wear the shoes—designed by Converse and Keds— that were so prized by athletes, popularizing the idea among young fans that sneakers could be worn off the sports field.

At the same time, other subcultures adopted sneakers, motivated by the same desire to reject convention. Whether worn by hippies, skaters, or even rock stars, they were paired with jeans, and television and the media helped spread the word: in 1971, Mick Jagger got married in a pair of Chuck Taylor All Stars. Gradually, sneakers took over the streets. In New York's underprivileged neighborhoods, they were practically a vital fashion accessory.

Guess What ? The United States has always been the epicenter of the sneaker's various incarnations, but Americans weren't the only ones setting the trends. In the United Kingdom, in the late 1970s, soccer fans adopted their own casual style, abandoning the distinctive looks that characterized the 1960s, such as skinheads, in order to escape police attention. At first, they wore the sleekest models by Adidas and Reebok, then lesser-known brands brought back from their travels in Europe, to perfect their boy-next-door outfits. Their casual style has endured and can still be seen in the stands today.

Field

Facing page, left
Marilyn Monroe and Keith Andes in Fritz Lang's 1952 movie *Clash by Night*. Monroe is wearing Keds' iconic model, the Champion.

Facing page, right
English students wearing sneakers as casual wear, 1986.

Right
English football hooligans associated with West Ham United FC in Nick Love's 2009 movie *The Firm*.

Hip-Hop:
And Then There Was

Although sneakers had already been repurposed, they really became a fashion accessory when they were picked up by the world of hip-hop.

Hip-hop, which encompasses various creative styles—from MCing, to graffiti, to break-dance—appeared in the early 1970s in New York's inner-city neighborhoods. Like any subculture, clothing was used as a way to create an identity within a hostile society. Hip-hop artists borrowed from different dress codes and references, but when it came to

Style

shoes, sneakers were it. Break-dancers, or
"B-boys," were the first to wear sneakers, for
the simple reason that they were the most
comfortable shoes for dancing. But form
quickly overtook function, and sneakers
came to define hip-hop style.

Adidas Superstar and Puma Suede—both
sturdy and easy to customize—were popular
with break-dancers, who built their outfits
around their shoes. It was about expressing
their personality and appearing "fresh." Nike
grasped the idea of sneaker-as-statement
with the Air Force 1 and Jordan lines, which
were both immediately adopted as
streetwear. In 1986, the phenomenon went
global with the help of rap group Run-DMC,
whose album *Raising Hell* was the first
worldwide success in the genre. The group's
members rejected the pop aesthetic that
record companies imposed on artists and
insisted on wearing their own clothes,
versions of contemporary streetwear:
Kangol bucket hats, Cazal glasses, Double
Goose jackets, Lee jeans, and, above all,
Superstar sneakers worn without laces—a
reference to the practice of removing laces
from inmates in US prisons.

Run-DMC's loyalty to the Three Stripes even
went as far as dedicating a song to their
much loved sneakers: "My Adidas." The hit
created a veritable craze for the German
brand, which eventually offered the crew an
endorsement deal, the first partnership
signed between a manufacturer and a non-
athlete. Using the Run-DMC model, many
artists began championing their favorite
brands, and sneakers became even more
popular as rap gained more listeners around
the world. Sportswear giants could have
capitalized on the success of rappers in the
1990s, but they didn't want to be associated
with the gangsta style of the time. Sneaker
manufacturers waited until the following

decade to pursue partnerships, when a new, less inflammatory music scene emerged.

Reebok was the first to make waves: in 2003, it enlisted Jay-Z (the S. Carter), 50 Cent (the G Unit), and Pharrell Williams (the Ice Cream) to collaborate on signature designs. The initial designs created a sensation and confirmed the artists' foresight, but long-term success still remained out of reach. It was not until later, with a certain Kanye West, that things came full circle. There is a loose parallel between rap artists and sneakers: both made the transition, at the same time, from underground to mass culture.

"Adidas can never even buy this promotion we give 'em…. 'My Adidas' is on the charts for six weeks…. It's going to the top. So give us a million dollars!" When Run-DMC were videoed backstage talking about the success of their song, they certainly didn't expect to see a contract materialize. But after the company's marketing director saw fans waving their Adidas Superstars at a Run-DMC concert, Adidas offered them the million dollars they had jokingly demanded—an amount that turned out to be peanuts compared to the profits made by the German brand.

Below
LL Cool J (for "Ladies Love Cool James"), star of the early hip-hop scene, 1987.

Facing page
A scene from Joel Silberg's 1984 movie *Breakin'*.

The 1980s:

Left
A break-dancer on a street in New York, 1981. He wears a Kangol bob, an icon of street culture popularized by American rappers in the 1980s.

Facing page
This ad ran in US magazines when the Air Jordan 2 was released in 1986. The luxurious model was made in Italy and marked the disappearance of the Swoosh logo from the Air Jordan line.

The 1980s gave rise to sneaker culture. This decade was the point of convergence between subcultures and athletic innovations, and sneakers were elevated to cult status.

The 1980s: carefree, creative, and decadent—words that could also be used to describe the sneaker scene. One explanation for the boom is the sneaker's adoption by the fast-rising world of hip-hop, but the sneaker revolution, which began in the United States, took place in a much larger context. Sports grew more popular in the 1980s, and with this came a cult of appearances and the body. Gym memberships soared and running went mainstream as people strove to sculpt their bodies, encouraged by an increasingly diverse and prevalent television media. As the first music channel, MTV, appeared and began broadcasting rap videos and the style

The Golden Era That Changed Everything

of its first icons, ESPN helped to make athletes into celebrities and brought sports like basketball to a wider audience.

In response to this unprecedented exposure, sportswear manufacturers competed fiercely to sign the most talented athletes and to offer ever higher-performing products for popular sports. Reebok's Freestyle, designed for fitness, was immensely successful, as was its Pump technology. Adidas released the Torsion, and Nike played its cards right: the Air

Force 1, the Dunk, and the Air Max line were all released in the 1980s. However, it was by enlisting the up-and-coming Michael Jordan for a signature line in 1984 that the Nike Swoosh made history.

The Jordan line was a game changer in many ways, but most of all it symbolized a new approach to design. Up until then, sneakers had been created solely for athletic performance; now Nike combined athletics with aesthetics, using all-new forms and

materials. The company also reinvented sports marketing with brilliant commercials. The storytelling in some went so far as to rewrite history, like the ad for the Air Jordan 1 Bred: the shoes were prohibited by the NBA's dress code, and Michael Jordan was supposedly fined for wearing them—but he never actually wore them at an NBA game. The popularity of the line was reinforced by memorable appearances on the small and big screens, including Spike Lee's *Do the Right Thing*, and grew as His Airness became a living legend on the courts.

The shoes were so popular that there were reports of people being mugged for their sneakers with the Jumpman logo. The line introduced the concept of the series—a new pair was released each year—which fanned the flames, and other brands used the model as a jumping-off point for new strategies and partnerships. Their successful experiments attracted the first collectors and laid the foundation for today's sneaker game (see Guess What?). Even the luxury industry, sensing the change in the air, began to take an interest in kicks: following in the footsteps

of pioneer Karl Lagerfeld, Gucci released the Tennis in 1984 and with it the concept of luxury sneakers. Ultimately, the craziness of the 1980s not only spurred the sneaker's transition from the courts to the streets, but also saw the birth of a new cult.

Guess What ? Nike commercialized the Air Force 1 in 1982, but in keeping with the company's strategy at the time, it stopped production two years later in favor of new product releases. On the East Coast of the United States, however, the shoe known as the "Uptown" achieved grail status. Sensing this shortage on the streets, three managers of stores in Baltimore, who would become known as "The Three Amigos," convinced Nike to supply them with exclusive colorways, which were snapped up immediately. This was a historic moment for the industry: it was the first collaboration between a manufacturer and a retailer, the first limited-edition production. It was so successful that the Air Force 1 was rereleased in 1986.

Facing page
American actor and director
Spike Lee during filming of
Do the Right Thing. Released
in 1989, the cult movie
depicts the daily life of the
residents of a working-class
neighborhood in Brooklyn.

Right
Times Square, New York,
1987. The boom box was
essential to rap and hip-
hop culture in the 1980s.

The 1980s were foundational, but the following decade was just as important in the history of sneakers. And for good reason: this is when the market proliferated and gave rise to a brand-new category: lifestyle.

In the days before the Internet, local trends were slow to spread internationally. The revolution that had taken place in the 1980s in the United States, when sneakers became fashion accessories, was not exported until the 1990s. The craze caught on in a similar way—through a combination of commercially successful rap music and the democratization of sports—but resulted in distinct styles.

The
1990s:

The majority of kids favored running shoes. Running had a second major boom in the 1990s, and manufacturers competed with each other to innovate and produce ever bolder designs. Nike carried the day with its Air Max lines. Individual models resonated with certain geographical regions and established deep cultural ties: the United Kingdom fell in love with the Air Max 90; Japan with the 95; Italy with the 97; and France with the Air Max Plus, which fans nicknamed *"la Requin"* (the Shark).

New urban consumption, encouraged by the popularization of skateboarding and a general shift toward more relaxed conventions, most notably "casual Friday," finally roused the industry. Manufacturers began to consider lifestyle a market in its own right and, for the first time, sneakers were made for daily life, not just for sports use. This sector quickly overtook performance in terms of production volume and sales.

Facing page
The Graffiti Hall of Fame, Harlem, 1991. The space is located in the courtyard of a local school. It was opened through the efforts of local activists to offer young graffiti artists a space for expression.

Above
Saint-Denis, in the northern suburbs of Paris, France, 1990.

The Lifestyle Decade

To keep the category thriving, experiments carried out in the 1980s became long-term strategies. Rereleases proliferated, like the return of the Air Jordan 1 in 1994, marking a break with manufacturers' traditional tactic of continuously releasing new products, and brands developed limited-edition collaborations or exclusive special editions in specific regions. Puma paved the way for luxury collaborations by inviting Jil Sander to codesign a collection in 1998. The stage was set for the arrival of the new millennium, when the sneaker would become a worldwide phenomenon.

Guess What ? Six hundred percent! That's how much sales of Nike shoes increased in the United Kingdom during the 1990s, and proof of the company's international appeal, which has enabled it to become the world leader in sportswear.

"For a long time,
the boundaries

Maximilien N'Tary-Calaffard, sneaker historian

Maximilien N'Tary-Calaffard has been a sneakerhead since he was a kid and has managed to turn his hobby into a profession. He now works as a consultant, journalist, and researcher, as he completes a thesis on digital influence on the sneaker market as part of a doctorate at the Sorbonne, the Institut Français de la Mode, and Columbia University. We sat down with him for a more historical perspective.

Basketball and hip-hop are often considered as the factors that changed the fate of sneakers and elevated them to cult status. But other groups had already adopted the shoes before then. What or who played a role in turning them into a bigger phenomenon?

Sneakers had been popularized off the sports fields since the emergence of the Ivy League fad and the university look of the 1950s in the United States. People also forget that before basketball there were several sports that brought sneakers into daily life: running, tennis, and aerobics, between the mid-1960s and the early 1980s. In the 1960s, road running became a subculture in its own right, and brands produced shoes to meet this demand. Over the following decade, people snapped up signature collections by tennis players like Björn Borg. When fitness took off, women wore their sneakers from the gym to the office. Hip-hop and basketball elevated sneakers to cult status in the streets. Basketball was the preferred sport of African Americans in the late 1960s and it could be played in the streets. So you would see sneakers promoted by the big NBA stars in every inner city.

They became far more widespread than the tennis or running shoes made popular by the epiphenomena of country clubs or jogging in California, which attracted a diametrically opposed population. This unprecedented scale is what differentiated basketball from previous appropriations of the sneaker, compounded by hip-hop culture, which was driven by the same population.

How do you explain the fact that sportswear brands were resistant to other uses for their products, and to their lifestyle potential, for so long?

It was very hard to grasp these other uses. Today, each company has a culture department, but for a long time the boundaries were clear. If you liked sports, you went to a stadium. Apart from running and basketball, you had to be affiliated with a federation to play a sport. So for the decision-makers at a sportswear brand, it was difficult to recognize, let alone understand, what was happening outside the lines! Jordan and Run-DMC changed the game in the mid-1980s. But even these feats didn't necessarily indicate a change of heart: Adidas more or less "put up with" its partnership with Run-DMC—it was the group who pushed for it—and the idea for

"Hip-hop and basketball elevated sneakers to cult status in the streets."

Jordan was driven by marketing expert Sonny Vaccaro. At that time, what was needed was someone to think beyond the sport in order to usher in something fresh, just as Reebok did with the aerobic shoe: an agent on the West Coast made the selfless suggestion after he visited his wife's gym and noticed a craze for aerobics, as well

were clear."

as a lack of dedicated footwear. Despite these successful examples, the lifestyle market took time to develop, even at Nike, where performance remained the focus until the creation of an NRG (for "Energy") department in 2005.

"The lifestyle market took time to develop, even at Nike."

When would you say design became as important as performance in brands' creative process?

In 1988, with the release of the Air Jordan 3. The Air Jordan 2 had been designed with fashion in mind, but it was a flop, and Michael Jordan wanted to leave Nike. Tinker Hatfield salvaged the operation, along with the company, which was once again on the verge of bankruptcy, by proposing something totally ground-breaking in terms of design: the Jumpman logo and visible air bubble. MJ loved it, it was a huge success, the American public was won over, and Nike was back in the spotlight. There truly is a before and after the Air Jordan 3, which triggered the war of visible technology. Before that, brands would say their shoes had this or that competitive advantage, but you couldn't see it. Now it was visible: Nike revealed its air bubble; Reebok developed the Pump system; Converse introduced the

Wave system; Adidas released the Torsion system; and Puma invented the Disc system. From there, music icons started wearing different models—appropriation, again—and the whole thing came full circle.

And when did most people stop seeing the sneaker as just a sports shoe?

In the late 1990s, when casual wear emerged; bankers decided that on Fridays, they could wear chinos and Oxford shirts to the office, with boat shoes or sneakers—plain ones, but sneakers nevertheless. The phenomenon grew, was widely adopted, and sneakers became socially acceptable. I experienced this myself: I graduated high school in 1992, before going to prep school for Sciences Po, where jeans and sneakers were forbidden. When I worked at GAP in 1998, the only sneakers allowed were Converse. And then in 2000, that was it—there were no more limits!

For a long time, sneakers were a symbol of rebellion. Do they still convey this significance now that they have gone mainstream?

No, sneakers have entirely lost this symbolism. Some shoes have certain connotations, and they are still used as signs of belonging to certain subcultures. But since the general public is not aware of these codes, mainstream wearers can wear the product just because they like the style, without realizing the secondary meaning. I'm thinking of the Adidas Samba, which was worn by members of the "casual" and skinhead movements, or the ultimate subculture shoe, the Converse All Star, which you'll find in every musical trend throughout the decades and is adored by the public. Ultimately, the more a pair of sneakers is worn and becomes popular, the less significance it has. But that goes for all products, it's part of their life cycle. As they reach a larger public, sneakers lose their essence, but there will always be a group that will wear them for what they once stood for.

Facing page

Vincent Cassel, Saïd Taghmaoui, and Hubert Koundé in *Hate*. Mathieu Kassovitz's 1995 film recounts the tribulations of a group of friends in a housing project in the Paris suburbs.

Below

A break-dance demonstration at L'Affranchi. Since its creation in 1996, this music complex in Marseilles has been a mecca for French rap and hip-hop, and launched the careers of artists like Soprano, Abd Al Malik, and Kery James.

Brand
and Mod

s
els

The sneaker market is driven
by manufacturers, which have
become veritable institutions.
Some have been around for more
than a century, and their stories
form part of a wider history of
making sports shoes to improve
performance. This frantic race
for innovation and increased
performance produced designs
that are now household names.
Let's take a look at the brands
and models that defined, are
defining, and will continue to
define sneaker culture.

Above
Steve Prefontaine crossing the finish line at the Modesto Relay in California in 1975, several months before his death in a car accident.

The Cortez—the first model to bear the Swoosh logo—appealed to runners because of its innovative herringbone sole. Steve Prefontaine wore the shoes at the Munich Olympics in 1972, the ideal launch pad for the brand. Nike continued to build a solid reputation in track and field with the Waffle Trainer, released the following year, while expanding into other sports like basketball, which was rapidly becoming popular.

Despite the introduction of classics like the Blazer and Air Force 1, Nike was unable to shake its image of a white, middle-class brand, and found itself on the verge of bankruptcy. The company took a gamble in 1984 when it invested in a signature line with the NBA's up-and-coming Michael Jordan, which put the business back on track. Even better: Nike's success spread beyond the United States, the company's designs were appropriated by different subcultures and acquired cultural cachet, and the emergence of limited editions attracted the first sneaker collectors. The release of the Air Max line in

Nike: The Undisputable Num

Nike is the world's leading sportswear manufacturer. Today worth over $100 billion, the American brand had to fight hard to unseat its European predecessors and competitors.

Nike was officially established in 1971 in Beaverton, Oregon. But the brand actually got its start in 1964, when founders Philip Knight and Bill Bowerman, both track and field enthusiasts, created Blue Ribbon Sports—a company they used to market running shoes made by the first incarnation of Asics, Onitsuka. They renamed the company Nike when they started designing their own running shoes.

1987 put the company in an advantageous position ahead of the lifestyle shift in the 1990s, which would make Nike the leading sportswear company.

While the brand still innovates for athletes with advances like the Flyknit technology that it unveiled in 2012, today Nike attracts sneakerheads with reinterpretations of iconic models and collaborations with prominent designers, from Chitose Abe to Travis Scott. Couple that with intelligent marketing and it's no wonder Nikes always sell out, leaving little room for competitors in the sneaker game.

27

Guess What?

Nike was named after the Greek goddess of victory, and the famous comma-shaped Swoosh is a stylized representation of the goddess's wings. Now one of the most recognizable logos in the world, it was designed at the last minute and was chosen half-heartedly. In a rush to launch their first collection, the founders hired a graphic design student, Carolyn Davidson, and paid her just thirty-five dollars.

ber One

Above, left
Bill Bowerman, cofounder of Nike, in his first workshop. Coach of the University of Oregon track and field team and very aware of the needs of runners, he came up with the first great Swoosh designs.

Above, right
The Nike Cortez—the first sneaker to bear the Swoosh logo—was released in 1972, but was created several years earlier with Onitsuka (see Guess What? p. 75).

Right
This ad ran throughout the United States in the 1980s.

The Models:

N

1972
Cortez

Before it became Forrest Gump's favorite sneaker, the Cortez marked Nike's auspicious debut. Released when the brand was established in the early 1970s, it revolutionized running, with its herringbone sole, and forged the brand's reputation. The Cortez later became a lifestyle model with California flair.

1973
Blazer

The Blazer was the first milestone in Nike's long relationship with basketball. Introduced in 1973 to help the brand break into this promising market and compete with Adidas and Converse, the high-top took off on the courts before skaters adopted it. Its simple design is the secret to its timeless appeal.

1982
Air Force 1

Nike's best-selling model was created by designer Bruce Kilgore and named after the US presidential plane, Air Force 1. Introduced in 1982 as a shoe for basketball, the design was popularized by rap artists and quickly caught on beyond the courts to become a casual-wear basic worn around the world.

ike

1985

Dunk

Propelled to stardom by high-profile collaborations with celebrities like Travis Scott, the Dunk is currently one of Nike's star models. Released in the company's basketball catalog in 1985, a few months after the Air Jordan 1, which was similar in appearance—both shoes were designed by Peter Moore—the Dunk found great success among skaters. In 2002, a version designed specifically for skateboarding was released and became iconic: the Nike SB Dunk.

1987

Air Max 1...

This symbol of Nike's success in the lifestyle market was initially created to revitalize the company's line of running shoes in 1987. But Tinker Hatfield's revolutionary design, featuring a cut-out sole that revealed the Air technology, appealed to more than athletes. The Air Max 1 became a fixture on the streets, as did the rest of the Air Max line that followed.

... and every other Air Max model

Launched by the Air Max 1, the Air Max line is packed with models that all followed a similar trajectory. Initially intended for running, the increasingly bold designs of the Air Max 90, 95, 97, and Air Max Plus have meant they have all been adopted as casual wear, strengthening Nike's position as the world's number-one sportswear manufacturer.

violated the NBA's strict uniform rules, Nike developed a skillful marketing campaign with a transgressive messaging approach that appealed to young fans. The Air Jordan 1 was a hit, and united fans beyond the courts.

This success was repeated each year when a new pair was released and worn by His Airness for the season. Buoyed by the star's popularity as well as by appearances on TV and in the movies, the sneakers were adopted by different subcultures, who imbued them with non-athletic significance and created a true cultural legend. After the Air Jordan 1, the Air Jordan 3, 4, and 11 are among the most iconic sneakers in history.

Today, the line comprises thirty-six models, largely made up of rereleases. Jordan became an independent brand in 1997, but remains a subsidiary of Nike. Jordan draws on the brand's prestigious pool of collaborators, while spreading its own wings through novel partnerships, such as

Jordan: The Other Nik Empire

Jordan is a subsidiary of Nike, named for the legendary basketball player Michael Jordan. Established in 1984 as the athlete's signature line, it produced some of the most iconic sneakers in history.

It was 1984, and twenty-one-year-old Michael Jordan was about to be discovered by the NBA. At the same time, the rookie signed an unprecedented contract with Nike that included shoes named after him, a clothing line, and royalties of 25 percent on each article sold. It effectively reinvented the endorsement contract, sports marketing, and sneaker design.

The Air Jordan 1, which launched the line, broke all the rules when it was released in 1985, with a unique design and bold color combinations based on the red, black, and white of Michael Jordan's team, the Chicago Bulls. When one of the colorways the one with Paris Saint-Germain Football Club, making it one of the world's leading sportswear manufacturers.

Guess What?

Initially, Michael Jordan didn't want to partner with Nike; he didn't like its products. But negotiations with his preferred brand, Adidas, and other hopefuls fell through. Encouraged by his mother, Deloris, His Airness ended up signing with the Swoosh. Despite his lucrative contract, he remained unconvinced, and Jordan, disappointed by the first couple of designs, considered jumping ship on more than one occasion. That is, until Tinker Hatfield finally won him over with the Air Jordan 3.

Facing page
Michael Jordan, aged twenty-two, and the Air Jordan 1 designed by Peter Moore, in the Chicago Bulls colorway.

Right
Michael Jordan at his first Slam Dunk contest organized by the NBA, in 1985. He ultimately lost to Dominique Wilkins, but had his revenge when he won the 1987 and 1988 competitions.

Below
An ad for the release of the Air Jordan 1, 1985.

WHO SAID MAN WAS NOT MEANT TO FLY.

The Models:

Jo

1985

Air Jordan 1

The Air Jordan 1 was the very first Jordan design and is the most representative of the line. Released in 1985, it was immediately popular for its radical design and bold colors. Now available in several versions—Low, Mid, and the original High—the AJ1 remains Jordan's star model and is often reinterpreted by the brand.

1988

Air Jordan 3

This is the model that convinced His Airness to stay with Nike. It was Tinker Hatfield's first design for Jordan, and when it was released in 1988 it did more than just win over MJ and other basketball players: with a visible Air bubble, an original cement print, and the all-new Jumpman logo—MJ doing a slam dunk—the design also won over the fashion crowd. And it went down in history.

rdan

1989
Air Jordan 4

The Air Jordan 4, based on the Air Jordan 3 that MJ liked so much, was designed to give the player increased flexibility and cushioning, symbolized by the more pronounced Air bubble and grids made of thermoplastic elastomer on the upper. As popular on the streets as its predecessor, the AJ4 is now one of the brand's preferred models for limited editions and collaborations.

1990
Air Jordan 5

Released in 1990, the fifth shoe in the line was equipped with better technology and cutting-edge design. Tinker Hatfield, comparing MJ's movements to those of a fighter jet, drew inspiration from the P-51 Mustang, evident in the flames on the sole. A reflective tongue, lace lock, and translucent outsole once again shook up aesthetics on the courts.

1995
Air Jordan 11

This was Michael Jordan's favorite model. The Air Jordan 11 stood out from the rest of the collection and generated a huge buzz when it was released in 1995. Its unique design was characterized by undulating lines on the upper and a construction that combined soft and patent leather, textured nylon, and neoprene. It remains one of the most popular designs in the brand's catalog.

Adidas was created in 1949, but its origins date thirty years earlier, when the founder opened his first sports shoe factory. He was joined by his brother Rudolf, and the company Gebrüder Dassler Schuhfabrik ("the Dassler brothers' shoe factory") was created in 1924. It grew rapidly, but fraternal disputes rooted in lingering resentments from World War II led to its demise.

The brothers parted ways; Rudolf founded Puma in 1948 and, a year later, Adolf followed suit with Adidas, deriving the name from his nickname "Adi" and the first three letters of his last name. The brand immediately made a splash with the Samba, a design created for the 1950 FIFA World Cup in Brazil. Instantly successful with soccer players and track-and-field athletes, its popularity did not wane until the 1960s, when it became important to diversify.

Adidas developed the Stan Smith, a model intended for tennis players that would become an all-time bestseller. The Superstar followed close behind, and several noteworthy initiatives, like signing an endorsement deal with rap artists Run-DMC, solidified Adidas's popularity. But, overtaken on the NBA courts by competitors and wracked by infighting after the death of the company director, the German brand found itself on the verge of bankruptcy in the late 1980s. At this point, French businessman Bernard Tapie took over and gave the company a fresh start.

Adidas:

The German brand Adidas was founded in 1949 by Adolf Dassler. A pioneer in many ways, the brand with the three-stripe logo was for years the world's sportswear leader, specialized in designing timeless models.

Adidas offered Yohji Yamamoto a line in 2002, pioneering the union between sportswear and high fashion—a niche the manufacturer continued to cultivate through partnerships with Stella McCartney, then Raf Simons, and finally Yeezy in 2013. This cult collaboration long gave the company a prime position on the sneaker market. The label's dissolution in 2022 caused Adidas to lose significant revenue, and the brand now intends to bounce back with new collaborations with designers. At the same time, Adidas remains at the cutting edge of innovation with its Boost and Futurecraft 4D technology, and appears to be spearheading a sustainable approach, keeping it hot on Nike's heels.

Facing page
Adolf Dassler in the
Gebrüder Dassler
Schuhfabrik ("the Dassler
brothers' shoe factory"),
founded in 1924.

Above
A still from Rick Rubin's
1988 movie *Tougher
Than Leather*; its release
coincided with that of Run-
DMC's eponymous album.

Below
Adolf Dassler, 1973.

Timeless

Guess What? "The brand with the three stripes" is Adidas's world-renowned nickname, a reference to the three parallel lines emblazoned on its products. But the brand didn't create the signature logo—Finnish brand Karhu did. The German manufacturer bought the logo in 1951 for the equivalent of about $1,600—and two bottles of whisky. Good stuff, by all accounts!

The Models:

A

1950
Samba

The model that launched Adidas also established the brand's sleek aesthetic. Initially created to provide traction on frozen European ground, the Samba was so named in order to introduce it to the world at the 1950 FIFA World Cup in Brazil. The model has been through several iterations, including a lifestyle version that still enjoys mainstream popularity.

1964
Stan Smith

The Stan Smith is Adidas's bestseller: more than one hundred million pairs have been sold since 1978, the year the shoe was renamed for the American tennis player whose portrait appears on the tongue (from 1964 to 1978, it was called the Robert Haillet, after the French tennis player who designed the shoe). Initially intended for wear on the tennis courts, today the sneaker is the very definition of classic style.

adidas

1966
Gazelle

Released in the late 1960s, the Gazelle—swift and graceful, like its namesake—was the first multisport sneaker. The design, characterized by a suede upper, was developed to adapt to all sports, but once again the street and different subcultures popularized the model, which has become timeless.

1969
Superstar

Adidas's other big hit is immediately recognizable by its rubber shell toe. The Superstar was designed for basketball and appealed to NBA players when it was released in 1969. The hip-hop crowd gave it a second wind in the 1980s, especially Run-DMC, who made it legendary in street culture.

2015
Ultra Boost

The Boost technology revolutionized the market with a midsole made of thermoplastic polyurethane particles expanded around tiny air pockets. The Ultra Boost running shoe, one of the brand's bestsellers, was named for this comfort-boosting technology, and a new version is released each year.

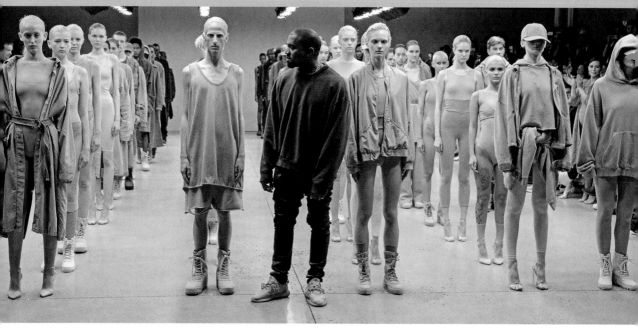

Yeezy: Avant- Garde

The Yeezy brand was created by Kanye West in collaboration with Adidas. It allowed the rapper to continue the revolution he had begun with Nike, design new classics, and forge a veritable empire—until his spectacular fall from grace.

The most influential artist of the past decade, West didn't earn the title through his musical production alone, but also through his position in the world of fashion and sneakers. A creative who knows no limits, the rapper delivered his first official collaboration in 2007, with the Tokyo-based brand Bape, before becoming the first non-athlete to sign a sneaker partnership with Nike two years later.

West dubbed his sneakers "Yeezy," like his nickname. With designs that paid tribute to Nike's heritage while embracing futuristic silhouettes, the Air Yeezy 1 and 2 immediately

established West as an avant-garde designer. The sharp aesthetics and limited quantities, as well as the rapper's popularity and his skillful mastery of teasing on social media, were the ingredients for an unprecedented success. But his relationship with Nike turned sour. The artist wanted royalties in addition to a contract, and it was Adidas who promised him this, along with greater creative freedom.

In 2013, the rapper left for Nike's rival and launched the collaborative line Yeezy. He waited almost two years to release his first sneaker, the 750—a direct descendant of his previous creations. Mocked on social media when it was first unveiled, the model sold out in seconds. The same happened with the models that followed, from the 350 to the 700, not forgetting the Slide, which were all instantly embraced by sneakerheads as classics. Yeezy drops increased over time and the brand was valued at $3 billion dollars in 2021—before the bubble burst the following year.

An impulsive and controversial figure, Kanye West began accusing his associate, Adidas, of plagiarism, of making strategic decisions without his consent, and, more broadly, of failing to respect their contract, expressing his wish to go it alone. His increasingly contentious stance reached a head when he made anti-Semitic remarks, and Adidas eventually ended the partnership, closing a chapter in sneaker history. This denouement hasn't been easy for either party: while the German sportswear maker has suffered staggering revenue losses, Ye has been left more alone than ever, and his desire to develop a solo brand seems somewhat thwarted.

Facing page
Kanye West presenting the Yeezy Season 2 collection at New York Fashion Week in 2015.

Below
Portrait of Kanye West, taken during a party hosted by *Vanity Fair* following the 92nd Academy Awards in 2020.

Above
The unique, futuristic Yeezy NSLTD Boot.

Guess What ? Although the termination of his contract with Adidas might suggest otherwise, Kanye West has proved himself time and again to be a visionary entrepreneur and ingenious designer. When Nike refused to pay him royalties on the grounds that he was not a professional athlete, he walked out, claiming he was "the first hip-hop designer" and arguing that in the age of the Internet musicians had to position themselves as stars to diversify their revenue streams. No sooner said than done: rapper-designers are now legion, including at Nike—where they must be kicking themselves for letting the OG slip away.

The Models:

Y

2015

Adidas Yeezy Boost 750

The first sneaker to come out of the collaboration between Kanye and the German brand. West's touch is evident in the novel aesthetic, minimalist colors, and premium materials.

2015

Adidas Yeezy Boost 350

Yeezy's historic bestseller has since been released in multiple versions. The low-top sneaker is distinctive for its singular shape featuring a woven upper composed of Primeknit and a ribbed Boost sole.

YZY

eezy

2017

Adidas Yeezy Boost 700

This archetypal "dad shoe" by West's brand was another big hit. The elegant silhouette with a generous sole features a mix of technology to maximize comfort. The OG "Wave Runner" colorway, rereleased many times, remains the most emblematic.

2018

Adidas Yeezy 500

A mix of runner and dad shoe, the 500 impresses with its chunky sole, another sign of West's bold creative approach.

2019

Adidas Yeezy Slide

Basically, a pair of slide sandals—but a stylish pair of slide sandals. The hugely successful Yeezy Slide features sharp design epitomized by its ridged sole and unique one-piece EVA construction.

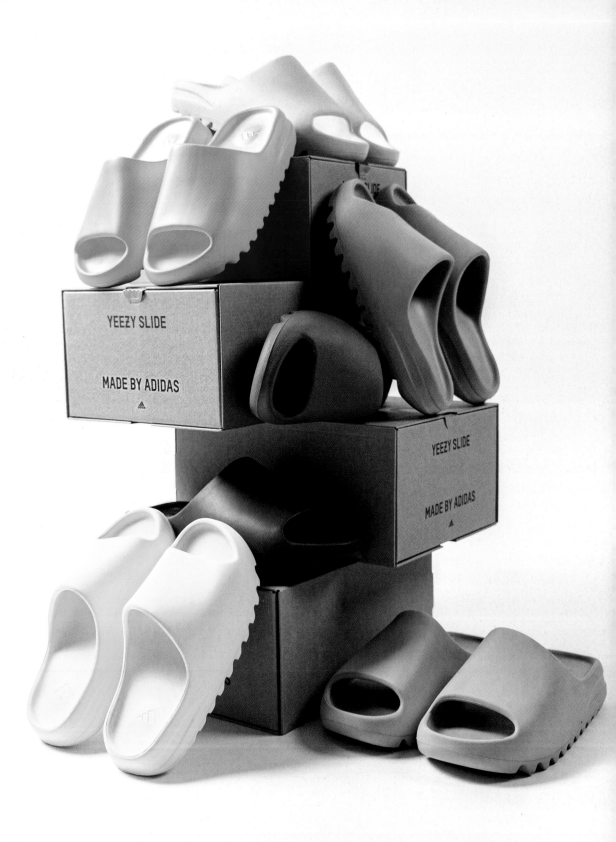

Puma was created following the notorious conflict between the Dassler brothers. After running a successful sports shoe factory together, which they founded in 1924, Adolf and Rudolf fell out after World War II and went their separate ways to set up their own labels: Adolf created Adidas, and Rudolf, Ruda, which quickly became Puma—a more accessible name with an evocative logo.

The company soon made a name for itself: from its inception in 1948, its Atom cleats trod the most prestigious playing fields. Recognizable in the 1950s for its signature feline and formstrip logo—the wave emblazoned on the side of its shoes—Puma released several successful soccer shoes, the Brasil and the King, which were notably worn by Pelé, and stood up to its old rival on the track.

In 1968, Tommie Smith raised his fist in protest on the winner's podium for the men's 200-meter sprint at the Mexico City Olympics, propelling Puma's Suede into the spotlight; it would become the company's classic model.

Pu

The Challenger

Founded after World War II by Rudolf Dassler, Puma is among the most recognizable historic sportswear makers. Although it may not make the most highly-prized sneakers, the brand with the leaping wild cat does have several classics to its name.

Modified five years later for NBA star Walt Frazier, the original spawned Puma's other great classic, the Clyde. The two styles were soon adopted by the emerging hip-hop crowd, and became part of a lifestyle and cultural shift.

In the 1990s, Puma skillfully responded to the boom in running with outstanding Trinomic and Disc technologies, and pioneered high-fashion collabs in 1998 with Jil Sander. But the brand lost ground when the lifestyle market emerged in the 2000s. Although it has fallen behind in the limited-edition sneaker niche, Puma has managed to maintain its position as one of the most profitable equipment manufacturers through its endorsements in high-level sports.

Facing page
Portrait of Rudolf Dassler, 1960s.

Left
The year of its creation, 1968, the Puma Suede featured in one of the most influential moments in sports history. Tommie Smith's raised fist made it a symbol of rebellion, which was later appropriated by the Black Panther movement.

Below
An ad for the Puma Clyde, a new version of the Suede designed for Walter "Clyde" Frazier, the first basketball player to have a shoe named after him, a decade before Michael Jordan.

ma:

Guess What ?

In the fierce war that they've been waging since their inception, Puma and Adidas had one opportunity to make peace: leading up to the 1970 FIFA World Cup, the two rivals agreed to stay away from the Brazilian star Pelé in order to avoid sky-high sponsorship bids. But Puma broke the "Pelé pact": the player wore a pair of King cleats during the competition and showed them off with a ploy that involved relacing his shoes before each kick-off. Adidas must have been furious when it found out!

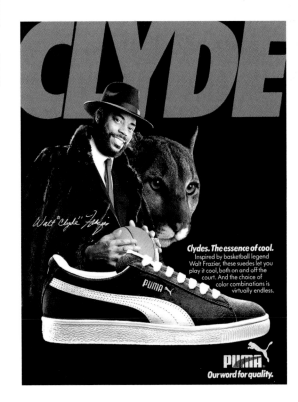

CLYDE

Walt "Clyde" Frazier

Clydes. The essence of cool.
Inspired by basketball legend Walt Frazier, these suedes let you play it cool, both on and off the court. And the choice of color combinations is virtually endless.

PUMA
Our word for quality.

The Models:

P

1968

Suede

Puma's greatest classic, unveiled in 1968 on the Olympic tracks under the name Crack, was immediately thrust into the spotlight with Tommie Smith's raised fist. The brand became legendary with its signature Suede (a reference to the suede leather upper), as it was later renamed, when B-boys adopted it in the 1980s.

1973

Clyde

Created for the basketball player Walt "Clyde" Frazier, whom the shoe is named after, this model is based on the Suede. The design is basically the same, except for a thinner sole and lower collar. Like its predecessor, it became a fixture in the hip-hop community and remains a timeless fashion staple.

uma

1986

RS

The RS series of lifestyle
sneakers is Puma's current
spearhead product line.
Named for the Running
System technology
developed in the 1980s,
the designs in the line are
symbols of a new on-trend,
retro-futurist approach.

1989

R698

The R698 was the first
model to feature Trinomic
technology, with its
characteristic hexagons
providing greater control
over movement, and has
been a favorite with runners
since its release in 1989.
This stylish running shoe
has also been the focus of
visionary collaborations,
notably with Ronnie Fieg,
the creator of Kith.

1993

Disc Blaze

Released in 1993, the Disc
Blaze featured Puma's new
Disc technology that replaced
laces with a single, twistable
disc. Combining innovation and
robust design, the silhouette
made an impression in its day.

Founded in Great Britain in the late nineteenth century, Reebok is the oldest of the leading sportswear makers. While it may have lost ground when it comes to endorsement deals, it remains a safe bet in the sneaker game thanks to its ever-classic models.

Reebok's date of creation is listed as 1958, but the company's history goes back much further: in 1895, the brand was registered in Bolton, England, under the name J. W. Foster & Sons, by its eponymous creator, which makes it the oldest of the sportswear giants. Initially, the company specialized in handcrafted spiked athletics shoes for track and field. They were so good that the best runners wore them at the 1924 Paris Olympics.

The name Reebok—a reference to a species of South African antelope—was adopted in 1958, as the company prepared to expand internationally. The manufacturer made inroads in the large US market without constituting a challenge for the leading brands. In the 1980s, the company made the profitable choice to diversify.

Reebok won over the booming aerobics market with the Freestyle, the first sneaker exclusively designed for women, which was released in 1982, and introduced multifunctional designs that later became classics. The NPC, Classic Leather, Workout, and Club C were all released in the early 1980s. At the same time, the company also adopted its famous vector logo and developed the revolutionary Pump technology, featuring inflatable cushions that delivered a custom fit. This enabled the brand to take a significant share of the basketball and tennis markets, making Reebok the world's number-one sportswear manufacturer at the time.

Soon overtaken by Nike, Reebok slumped and was eventually acquired by Adidas in 2005 for over $3 billion. Under the Three Stripes, the brand gradually refocused on fitness and reissued classics while launching limited editions in collaboration with prestigious brands such as Vetements, Maison Margiela, Pyer Moss, and Palace. Acquired in 2022 by the US company Authentic Brands Group, Reebok will likely take a new direction in the coming years.

Reebok: The Outsider

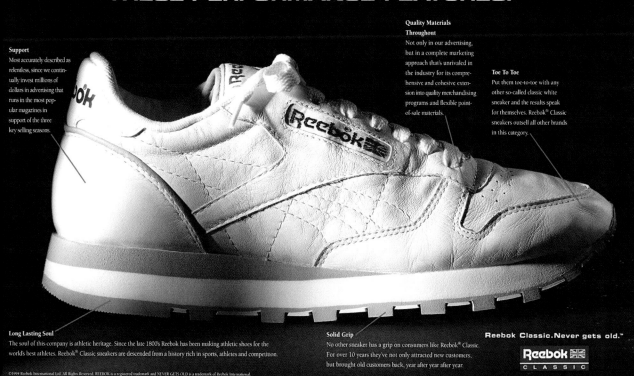

NO OTHER SNEAKER COMES WITH THESE PERFORMANCE FEATURES.

Support
Most accurately described as relentless, since we continually invest millions of dollars in advertising that runs in the most popular magazines in support of the three key selling seasons.

Quality Materials Throughout
Not only in our advertising, but in a complete marketing approach that's unrivaled in the industry for its comprehensive and cohesive extension into quality merchandising programs and flexible point-of-sale materials.

Toe To Toe
Put them toe-to-toe with any other so-called classic white sneaker and the results speak for themselves. Reebok® Classic sneakers outsell all other brands in this category.

Long Lasting Soul
The soul of this company is athletic heritage. Since the late 1800's Reebok has been making athletic shoes for the world's best athletes. Reebok® Classic sneakers are descended from a history rich in sports, athletes and competition.

Solid Grip
No other sneaker has a grip on consumers like Reebok® Classic. For over 10 years they've not only attracted new customers, but brought old customers back, year after year after year.

©1994 Reebok International Ltd. All Rights Reserved. REEBOK is a registered trademark and NEVER GETS OLD is a trademark of Reebok International.

Reebok Classic. Never gets old.™

Reebok ⌘
CLASSIC

Facing page
Portrait of Reebok CEO Paul Fireman, 1992. After purchasing the brand from Joe Foster in 1984, the American businessman significantly contributed to its growth as a sportswear leader.

Above
The essential Reebok Classic, introduced in 1983, became one of the brand's most iconic designs.

Below
An ad for the Reebok DMX 10, an iconic model created in 1997. A major new feature of the DMX was its airflow sole: a patented technological innovation that guaranteed excellent cushioning and better stability.

Guess What ?

Reebok could have been the first brand to release a Yeezy designed by Kanye West. In 2004, the rapper was introduced to Reebok by his friend Jay-Z, who was affiliated with the company, and designed a new model for them called Mascotte Trainer. It did not end well: according to someone involved in the project and close to West, Reebok marketed the pair without his permission or his signature, triggering the artist's ire and a complaint for breach of contract. The sneaker was withdrawn from the shelves and Reebok wrote a check to put an end to the dispute—and to what had been shaping up to be a profitable relationship.

Go to hell.
(And back again.)

An intelligent lifeform by Reebok

The Models:
Reek

1982

Freestyle

One of Reebok's most successful models, this hit established the brand as a pioneer in the 1980s fitness trend. At its peak, the very first sneaker designed for women and intended for indoor sports accounted for half of the brand's total footwear sales.

1983

Classic Leather

Reebok's emblematic model, the Classic Leather was introduced in 1983 as a running shoe, but soon became synonymous with lifestyle wear. Appreciated for its sleek look, high-quality materials, and accessible price, it was adopted by many underground cultures, and went on to become a mainstream bestseller and a truly timeless shoe.

ook

1992

Aztrek

In its day, Aztrek—archetype of the 1990s running shoe—managed to compete with the Nike Air Max. It's no surprise, then, that designer Christian Tresser was later hired by Nike to design the Air Max 97. Combining high-performing new technology and style, the Aztrek has enjoyed a well-deserved revival since 2018, thanks to the dad shoe trend.

1986

Club C

Reebok's other bestseller was designed in 1986 for tennis players. The Club C followed a similar trajectory to the Classic and shares several similarities with its predecessor—sleek lines, clean aesthetics, and an affordable price—making it another classic model.

1989

Pump

In response to an onslaught of technology from its competitors, Reebok introduced the Pump in 1989. Its namesake system, which inflates air cushions at the touch of a button on the tongue to deliver a personalized fit, was immediately successful. As cool as it was revolutionary, Pump technology has since appeared on many models, including the Instapump Fury, which is currently one of the brand's preferred models for collaborations.

The story goes that Converse was born out of an accident. When Marquis Mills Converse fell down a flight of stairs, he decided to create a non-slip shoe. He started his company in 1908 in Malden, Massachusetts, and initially sold lined boots with rubber soles. In 1915, the company began producing sports shoes.

The Non-Skid, designed for basketball and made of a canvas upper on a rubber sole, was created in 1917. It was renamed the All Star three years later; in 1934, Chuck Taylor, a basketball player who championed the model, added his name to the signature medallion logo. The Chuck Taylor All Star, which has remained virtually unchanged to this day, eventually became the best-selling sneaker of all time.

Converse dominated the market by pairing its first critical successes with significant investments in athlete sponsorship and major events: by the end of the 1950s,

Above
Earvin "Magic" Johnson and Larry Bird, 1984. Converse ambassadors and NBA nemeses in the 1980s, their rivalry played out against the backdrop of Celtics and Lakers games, and contributed greatly to the NBA's popularity.

Founded in 1908, Converse was one of the very first sportswear manufacturers. The company's history is inextricably linked to the saga of its ultimate classic, the Chuck Taylor, which went from being a star on the courts to a cross-generational cultural phenomenon.

Converse held an 80 percent share of the US athletic shoe market and 90 percent of professional basketball players wore the brand's products. Around this time, the Chuck Taylor became a fashion phenomenon. The greatest idols of pop and counter-culture—Elvis, James Dean, Mick Jagger, Kurt Cobain—wore the sneaker, and it was embraced by generations of teenagers.

Its status as icon and symbol of the American way of life did not prevent Converse from flagging. After its heyday on the courts in the 1980s, the brand filed for bankruptcy in 2001. It was ultimately acquired by Nike, who, with proven methods, modernized it through a series of rereleases and collaborations with brands such as Comme des Garçons, Off-White, and Golf le Fleur—just what was needed to enable the legendary Chuck Taylor All Star to endure and shine once again.

Made by Lewis Hughes-Batley

Made by Andrea Penaranda

verse: Classic

Above, left and right
Images from Converse's ad campaign "Made by You," launched in 2015 to celebrate fans of the legendary Chuck Taylor All Star from around the world.

Below
An ad campaign that ran in the United States in 1985, announcing the release of a range of new Chuck Taylor All Stars.

LIMOUSINES FOR YOUR FEET.
Converse All Stars® The original canvas high tops and oxfords in eighteen fun and flashy colors and prints for people who want to go places in style.

CONVERSE
Reach for the star

Guess What? As of 2014, one billion Chuck Taylor All Stars had been sold since the model was released. In 2015, the brand claimed to have sold one hundred million more, or 270,000 pairs every day—that's three every second! Converse's classic model is by far the best-selling sneaker in history.

The Models:
Conve

1917
Chuck Taylor All Star

Released in 1917 as the Non-Skid, the Chuck Taylor All Star has stridden across the decades without a wrinkle in its canvas or a scratch on its rubber soles. Not just the symbol of Converse, the iconic design is popular with generations both young and old. It is now available in a variety of high- and low-top versions.

1935
Jack Purcell

Named for the badminton player who created the design in 1935 for another brand, the Jack Purcell didn't join the Converse catalog until 1972, when the company bought the trademark. Similar to the Chuck Taylor in both materials and design, enhanced with a toe smile, it is now considered a classic.

erse

1974

One Star

To compete with Adidas and Puma, and their premium materials that bested canvas, Converse introduced the One Star in 1974. Although it was quickly replaced by the Pro Leather on the courts, this pair, with its central star, would become legendary once it was adopted by the 1990s grunge and skate scenes.

1976

Pro Leather

Introduced in 1976 as Converse's new premium b-ball shoe, the Pro leather—a high-top featuring the signature chevron—was popular with the biggest NBA stars of the day. Replaced by more recent models in the 1980s, it was revived by the hip-hop and skate communities.

2019

Run Star Hike

This recent Converse creation is a common sight on the streets. A reinterpretation of the Chuck Taylor designed in collaboration with JW Anderson, the Run Star Hike features the classic canvas upper rising from an imposing midsole and a serrated outsole, with, at the back, the signature star which emerges from the heel. When trend meets timelessness.

New Ba

One of the world's leading sportswear manufacturers, New Balance cultivates a distinctive image. With historic connections to running and a highly functional and quality-focused approach, the brand has also appealed to collectors in recent seasons.

Sneaker stories tend to start with an anecdote—and New Balance's begins with one man observing chickens. Noting their perfect balance, orthopedic shoemaker William R. Riley had the idea to create an insole that mimicked their three-claw support points, a "new balance" that inspired the brand name. The company was officially launched in Boston in 1906, selling products that supported the arch of the foot.

In 1938, the company, nicknamed NB, developed its first running shoe for a local running club. As the range of products expanded in the following decade to include shoes for baseball, tennis, and boxing, the company distinguished itself from the competition by refusing to sponsor athletes. It preferred to be chosen out of conviction. NB managed to attract a considerable number of athletes in the 1960s with its Trackster model—the first sneaker available in different widths.

Until then, the company had relied on the artisanal work of a six-person production team. But in 1972, New Balance expanded with the arrival of its current owner, Jim Davis. NB began exporting worldwide and built a reputation with the 320—the first model to feature the centrally placed "N"— before new models began to proliferate in the 1980s, when the company became

According to sneaker media, New Balance won the sneaker games in 2020 and 2021. Although "only" the fourth largest brand worldwide in terms of turnover, NB challenged Nike's position in the hearts of sneaker lovers by reissuing models from its archive and original creations with strong designs, all driven by first-class collaborations with the likes of Kith, Casablanca, JJJJound, Salehe Bembury, and Aimé Leon Dore.

Facing page
Dan MacBride, a member of the Boston running club the Brown Bag Harriers, wore the very first pair of New Balance sneakers for the Reddish Road Race in 1938. The model was made of kangaroo leather, known for being durable and lightweight.

Left
The first New Balance Arch store, at 2402 Massachusetts Avenue in Cambridge, Massachusetts.

Below
The famous "N" that has appeared on every one of the brand's shoes since the release of the New Balance 320 in 1976.

alance:
Distance Runner

recognized as an expert in performance running shoes.

The brand gradually gained popularity in the lifestyle category and became a symbol of the normcore style embodied by Steve Jobs. The company's limited editions, which appeared in the mid-2000s, also appealed to sneakerheads. Since then, they have appreciated NB's unfailing commitment to quality, apparent in its premium ranges made in the USA and in the UK, which differentiate it from other brands in the sector. And NB's excellence continues to impress.

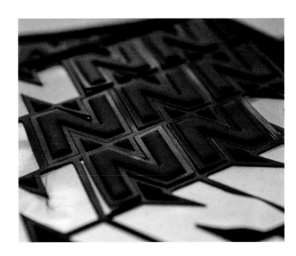

The Models:
New B

1982
New Balance 99X Series

In 1982, the 990 was released as the first sneaker in the 99X line, which includes all models that begin with 99—by far New Balance's most emblematic series. Premium materials, simple designs, and original gray colorways embodied NB's successful formula.

1988
New Balance 5 Series

The 5 Series also embodies the New Balance look. Introduced in 1988 with the 574—a technical running shoe with improved comfort—this line now features a number of models and remains popular for everyday wear.

alance

1989

New Balance 550

One of New Balance's biggest current successes is based on this design, recently unearthed from the brand's archives. Introduced in 1989 in the company's basketball catalog on the initiative of legendary designer Steven Smith, the 550 had yet to make an impression. In 2020, New York brand Aimé Leon Dore created a buzz around the shoe and inscribed its retro aesthetic into the contemporary fashion canon.

1993

New Balance 1500

This sleek running shoe is among the Boston brand's bestsellers and has been ever since it was released in 1993. Popularized by a number of celebrities who wore it for jogging, the 1500 was also NB's first major model used for collaborations.

2010

New Balance 2002R

Another comeback story: like the 550, the 2002R was a flop when it was released in 2010, mainly because of its high price. But like the 550, this dad shoe was dusted off in 2020 and revived through collabs. It's been a trendsetter ever since.

Asics:
Technology First

Asics was founded after World War II near Kobe, Japan. Known for the high technical quality of its products and innovations developed for athletes, the brand appealed to sneakerheads for the same reasons.

Before adopting the name Asics, the Japanese brand went by the name of its creator, Kihachiro Onitsuka, who started out in 1949 with the idea to produce basketball shoes. His first pair was remarkable for its innovative outer sole featuring suction cups inspired by octopus suckers. But Onitsuka's reputation grew with the release of its running shoes in 1953.

The brand took advantage of the Olympic Games to sponsor champion athletes, making a name for itself as a running-shoe specialist. The 1964 Tokyo Olympics created opportunities in new markets, especially the United States, where the brand was distributed by Nike's first incarnation, Blue Ribbon Sports. During the next Olympics, in Mexico City, Onitsuka introduced the signature stripes, dubbed the Mexico lines, that have appeared on its sneakers ever since.

In 1977, the company rebranded itself as Asics, the acronym for the Latin expression *anima sana in corpore sano* ("a sound mind in a sound body"), after a decade of expanding into other sports and developing innovations in the realm of running. In 1986, the brand's research culminated with the release of Gel technology to improve shock absorption and comfort, and the technology was added to Asics's iconic models. The Gel-Lyte, Gel-Saga, and Gel-Kayano running shoes, some of the brand's best-selling sneakers, were all released in the 1990s.

In the 2000s, Asics reached a wider audience due as much to publicity from Quentin Tarantino's film *Kill Bill* as to the creation of a lifestyle line that married technical quality and design—a combination the brand has come to symbolize. Limited-edition releases took care of the rest, with collaborators ranging from brands like Kith and Patta to the designer Kiko Kostadinov. Today, Asics is a key player in sneaker culture.

Guess What ?

Onitsuka played a major role in the creation of Nike—the founders got their start selling Onitsuka products. Together with the brand, the Americans designed a pair of sneakers in 1969 that they ended up developing in parallel under the Swoosh logo, unbeknownst to their Japanese partner. Onitsuka took the case to court, where it was ruled that both brands could market the same model—the Cortez for Nike and the Corsair for Onitsuka—resulting in the only sneaker to become a bestseller for two different brands.

Facing page, left
Kihachiro Onitsuka outside his first store in the 1950s.

Facing page, right
A prototype of the Marathon Tabi, the first shoe developed for marathon running. Released in 1953, the model sought to apply Japanese traditions to the legendary sporting event (*tabi* are typical Japanese shoes that separate the big toe from the others).

Above
Cover of the spring 1966 Onitsuka Tiger catalog featuring the 1968 Olympic Games in Mexico City. It announces the release of the iconic Onitsuka Tiger Mexico 66, the first model to feature the brand's signature stripes.

Below
A still from Quentin Tarantino's 2003 movie *Kill Bill*. Uma Thurman and her pair of Onitsuka Tiger Mexico 66s entered the pop culture canon.

The Models:

A.

1986

GT-II

The GT-II is a legend in the Asics catalog: it was the first design equipped with the famous Gel technology, the brand's first international release, and the basis for the brand's first collaboration in 2004. It was probably also the first pair to appeal to the everyday wearer due to its elegantly simple design.

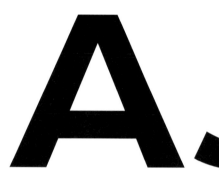

1990

Gel-Lyte III

Asics's flagship model conveys the brand's philosophy. Designed in 1990 to give runners maximum lightness, the Gel-Lyte really made an impression with its atypical design, embodied by its split tongue. The sneaker has since become the brand's preferred model for collaborations.

sics

2015
Gel-Quantum

One of Asics's latest releases, this is also one of its most popular. Introduced as a performance sneaker, the Quantum features visible Gel technology for the first time— the ideal response to the desires of lifestyle consumers seeking bold designs.

1991
Gel-Saga

Introduced in 1991 in the wake of the Gel-Lyte III, the Saga, named for the Nordic goddess, effectively combines performance and aesthetics. The model's clean lines appealed to a wide audience, making it one of Asics's bestsellers.

1993
Gel-Kayano

Less conventional than its predecessor, the Saga, the Kayano was introduced in 1993 as a performance running shoe intended to maximize comfort and protection during long-distance races. The sneaker's dynamic curves have also made it a popular streetwear basic, in its many iterations.

Vans is not a sportswear manufacturer per se, but the brand can hold its own among the sector's giants. From its success in skate culture to its immersion in the world of music, the California brand has one of the richest histories in the sneakerverse.

Vans was founded by brothers Paul and James Van Doren in 1966, in Anaheim, California. They wanted to make high-quality, accessible canvas shoes, and it wasn't long before they made a name for themselves with their first pair, the #44, which later became known as the Authentic. The design was wildly popular with local riders who liked its sturdiness and non-slip qualities.

As skate culture took off, California was at the epicenter. Vans embraced the movement and expanded as the sport grew in popularity. The number of followers increased in the 1970s, and the brand designed sneakers for them that remain some of its most iconic. From the Era to the Old Skool to the Sk8-Hi, each features improvements for skateboarding and now-familiar signature design elements, like the central jazz stripe and the Off the Wall logo.

Although it came out in 1977, the Slip-On would open up new horizons for Vans five years later, with the release of the movie *Fast Times at Ridgemont High*. Sean Penn wore the Checkerboard version, which

Vans:
Skate Star

became a worldwide phenomenon. But excellent sales couldn't cover the company's extensive, risky investments, and Vans went bankrupt in 1984. The brand was sold several times, until the VF Corporation group brought stability and a fresh approach in 2004.

Vans sneakers were adopted by various alternative music communities, from punk to rock to hip-hop, which appreciated the brand's many designs and patterns. So the company increased production of special editions with cultural significance. Pop figures like The Simpsons, artists, brands, and even couture labels such as Kenzo and Comme des Garçons have cosigned models with the brand, which is now firmly rooted in sneaker culture and appreciated by a wide audience.

Guess What? Vans was THE pioneer in customization, a wildly popular phenomenon today. The founders of the brand, whose initial credo was custom production, let their first customers choose colors and fabrics. Shoes were made the same day and sold for between just $2.29 and $4.49.

Facing page
Released in 1978, Vans Sk8-Hi were the first high-top skateboard shoes. This new design was intended to better protect the ankle, which was particularly exposed and prone to injury.

Above
A photograph taken at the Mangawhai Bowl Jam, one of the main skateboarding events in New Zealand, 2019.

Below
Sean Penn in *Fast Times at Ridgemont High*, released in 1982. The movie was instrumental in popularizing the Vans Slip-On and its checkerboard pattern.

The Models:
Var

1966

Authentic

Released as the #44 in 1966, the Authentic was the first sneaker developed by Vans. With simple, clean design, a canvas upper, and robust rubber sole, the model was quickly adopted by California skaters and remains popular today.

1976

Era

The Era was released in 1976—as the #95—and was clearly intended for skateboarders. It was created in collaboration with riders Tony Alva and Stacy Peralta, who modified the Authentic to make it even more efficient on the board, notably by adding a padded collar. This model has remained a success for decades on end.

VANS ®

S

1977

Old Skool

Despite its name, the Old Skool featured major innovations for 1977, when it was released: it was the first Vans design to feature leather details for greater durability and, most importantly, the first to feature the jazz stripe, a contrasting band on the side of the shoe that has become a signature of the brand.

1977

Slip-On

This is no doubt the most iconic Vans sneaker. Introduced in 1977, the Slip-On—a laid-back, lace-free model—became a worldwide hit when Sean Penn wore the cult Checkerboard version in *Fast Times at Ridgemont High*.

1978

Sk8-Hi

The Sk8-Hi was released in 1978, once again as a response to the needs of skateboarders. The high-top design covered the ankle, the area most prone to injury, and quickly became popular with skaters. It also gained a second life as an everyday shoe.

Other

Br

There's more to sneakers than big names. A host of other players are making waves in sneaker culture, whether they are small manufacturers or brands in related fields. Here's a non-exhaustive list of who to watch.

Saucony

This historic sports-shoe maker founded in 1898 in the United States became famous in the 1970s and '80s for making high-quality running shoes. The brand, well served by limited editions, has enjoyed a revival in the lifestyle market in recent seasons.

Mizuno

Japan's leading sportswear manufacturer, Mizuno has had a rich history in sports since its inception in 1906. The brand has also made a name for itself in the sneaker game, with assertive designs like the Sky Medal running shoe and recent avant-garde creations.

Fila

Fila, an Italian sportswear brand created in 1911, has gone through several iterations, from underwear specialist to tennis star sponsor to hip-hop brand popular for its Fitness model. After disappearing from the scene, Fila has made a comeback in recent seasons with its lifestyle sneakers and partnerships with fashion icons.

ands

Salomon

We could have cited Le Coq Sportif for a touch of French *je ne sais quoi*, but the rise of Salomon merits attention. Created in Annecy in 1947, the brand initially focused on skiing before a move to trail running. Its technically sophisticated models, regularly enhanced by collaborations, are now popular with the fashion-forward.

Diadora

Diadora—another Italian brand, founded in 1948—made a name for itself in soccer early on. Today, the brand is popular with collectors for its elegant, premium running shoes, which are regularly the result of collaborations.

Bape

Japanese streetwear brand Bape, founded in 1993 by the designer Nigo, made waves in sneaker culture with the release of Bape Sta: a low-top heavily inspired by the Nike Air Force 1. Pop colorways made it a classic in its own right.

Luxury

Luxury brands long poo-pooed sportswear, but they finally embraced the trend when it exploded in the 1980s. Now each one offers its own vision of the sneaker and inspires the industry with avant-garde designs.

Louis Vuitton

The brand made an initial impression with the imposing Archlight model, but Louis Vuitton really turned a corner with Virgil Abloh. From 2018 to his death in late 2021, the designer greatly expanded the French brand's range, drawing inspiration from skateboarding, running, hiking, and, of course, basketball, with the much-touted LV Trainer.

Balenciaga

The most influential brand of the past few seasons, Balenciaga has undeniable cachet in the sneaker market. From the Runner to the Speed to the Triple S—paragon of the chunky sneaker trend—the brand's models are each more voluminous and extravagant than the last, and they are all incredibly popular.

Gucci

This Italian brand was a pioneer in the luxury sneaker market. Karl Lagerfeld paved the way on the runway with the Chloé, but the Tennis really launched the concept in 1984. Since then, the brand has remained very active. Its Rhyton has been particularly successful.

Contenders

Dior

LVMH's other vanguard brand is not to be outdone in the sneaker market. Dior has also significantly developed its offerings under the leadership of Kim Jones, an art director inspired by street culture. His incredibly successful B23 has won over a large number of consumers who are not usually luxury shoppers, while his collab with Jordan will not be forgotten anytime soon.

Maison Margiela

Through a long-term collaboration with Reebok, Margiela transformed his signature Tabi split-toe shoes into sneakers. He has also influenced the industry through his own designs: his Replica—a reproduction of a 1970s sports shoe worn by the German army—became a classic upon its release in the 1990s and has inspired a slew of minimalist models.

Alexander McQueen

No list would be complete without the sneakers by the late British designer. A sort of voluminous Stan Smith, the Oversize has been one of the most popular high-fashion sneakers for years.

"Rationality
disappears
in the face of

Elie Costa, collector

Sneakers can become an all-consuming passion and result in an extravagant collection. But how? Elie Costa, who has one of the largest collections of Nike SB Dunk in Europe, gives his reasons—which often go beyond reason.

Where does your passion for sneakers come from, and how did you cultivate it to the point of becoming a collector?

In my case, it didn't develop through sports. I became interested in sneakers purely for the aesthetics. I remember my first obsession, in 2001. I begged and pleaded with my parents for a pair of Nike Air Max International. Then, in 2002, I was blown away by the Air Max Plus that a guy in my class had—a gray Shark with an orange swoosh and a cream sole that I found beautiful. We exchanged pairs during recess; he played soccer in my Reebok Classics while I showed off with his Nikes. Then I had another tantrum in front of my mother at Foot Locker and got my first pair. I didn't know anything about shoes at the time, but with the Shark, I entered the matrix. I was lucky to have access to the Internet early on and after typing in some keywords, I stumbled on a forum, rekins.com, that dealt only with Air Max Plus. There I met other fans, got myself an education, and, via the marketplace, my thirst for accumulation developed in the "catch them all" spirit of Pokemon. From there, it was buy, buy, buy—just Sharks, from 2002 to 2005–6. I became a collector pretty quickly. I wore my first purchases, but soon I caught the notorious "one to rock, one to stock" bug. Then sneakers.fr came online; I met new people and opened up to other models, like Jordan and Nike SB Dunk, for which I am now recognized as a collector.

Air Max Plus, Jordan, SB Dunk—these are all very different models. What drew you to certain shoes and not others? Rarity, value, or aesthetics, once again?

Aesthetics. When I think a pair is beautiful, I buy it. Regardless of hype, retail value, or even brand, for that matter, even if I do have a particular fondness for Nike. I have a lot of sneakers that no one likes. But I like them. It's not a competition. I don't do it for others, I don't do it for social media. I do it for myself, because it makes me happy. As early as 2012, I had a detailed wish list. I had shared with my contacts my desire to buy rare pairs that were already expensive and, given the context, they thought I was crazy. But there is an aim behind every collection—a thirst for knowledge, a thirst for accumulation.

"When I think a pair is beautiful, I buy it."

Speaking of which, how did you manage to build up your collection and where are you with it now?

As we speak, I have three hundred pairs in my collection. If I had kept everything, I would have six or seven hundred. I faced financial constraints early on, so I had to make concessions, what I considered to be real trade-offs. I sold pairs in order to buy others. To get my Nike SB Dunk Paris and Pigeon by City Pack, I gave up ninety-six pairs of Air Max Plus. Sometimes I did it with regret, to seize an opportunity. But that's how I was able to acquire ultrarare SB Dunks, in addition to the City Pack itself, like the Dunk × Michael Lau Friends & Family (there are only twenty-four pairs in the world), the Dunk × Stash (fifty pairs), the Dunk Freddy Krueger, etc. And I got lucky; great opportunities presented themselves. "The right place at the right time," as they say. That's a good way of describing how I was able to acquire the pairs I have. I've gotten them in some pretty crazy ways: paying four figures in cash to a guy I didn't know, who set up a meeting with me at an undisclosed location; trading on

passion."

Instagram with a guy based in Asia—I could so easily have gotten scammed! But rationality disappears in the face of passion. Let me give you an idea of just how much it has affected me: I rent an extra room to store my shoes. Is that not proof of a guy who's lost his mind? There's no denying it—collectors suffer from a sort of madness.

As a collector and an enthusiast, how do you decide which pairs to wear or to keep?

If I have the opportunity to double or triple a model, the question is moot. Otherwise, it depends on how much I'm going to pay. On the current market, a rare pair means an expensive pair. And I've gotten to the point where, if I pay a lot for a pair of sneakers, I won't wear them because I'd be afraid of damaging them. It's a little masochistic really, spending so much money on something you'll never enjoy. You buy the pair and it stays in its box. Which is at my house, stacked on another box, on top of another box. This is the compulsive collector speaking. I once bought a pair that I idolized, opened the box, thought "cool," closed it, and put it in a pile. Then I forgot about it until I sorted through my collection two years later! You move on. You get caught up in consumer society. You become a victim. It's a game: you buy, buy, buy. I often rediscover pairs that I've owned for over ten years, which can be worth a lot of money. And, of course, I have phases. For example, I don't wear Diadora much now. After thinking about it, I decided that I wouldn't wear them anymore, that the brand appealed to me less and less, and that those would be the pairs I sell next. They take up space, it's idle money, so I might as well recycle them for new pairs—it's a vicious circle. You don't spend money, it lies dormant on your shelves.

Have you ever calculated the value of your collection and been tempted to sell it?

For the past few years, I've kept a chart of all my purchases. For each model, I list the date, purchase price, and name, and include a photo. Given their value, I'm sitting on a small nest egg. If I were to sell my SB Dunk Paris, let's say at the lowest price reached at the most recent auctions—€82,000 (about $81,700/£71,700)—I will have made my entire collection profitable: three hundred pairs paid off in one go. If I sell my entire City Pack and a few more rare pairs like the SB Dunk Iron Maiden, the Michael Lau, and the Freddy Krueger, I'd have a solid deposit to buy a nice apartment.

"It's a game: you buy, buy, buy. I often rediscover pairs that I've owned for over ten years, which can be worth a lot of money."

I've already considered it because of the frustration this game creates, because of the fact that I'm not really in it anymore, because I'm reaching an age where priorities are different. It takes space, money, and time. I'm less involved today. There are too many releases and not as much creativity. Limited editions are overused and it's become very difficult to buy. So yes, I have seriously considered selling my collection, to the point of saying that I will first sell the "small" pairs and then the bigger pieces. Through my connections, I would have no trouble finding takers, people able to fly from the other side of the world to meet me with cash. The opportunity has already presented itself, but I've always refused. Because I do this out of passion, not for the money. And then I tell myself that I would be selling pairs that I could never see again. It would be impossible to get a pair of SB Dunk Paris back, for example. The fear of disappointment holds me back. So, ultimately, I think I will always be surrounded by at least a few boxes.

Facing page
The complete line-up of the legendary City Pack. Created by Nike's skateboard division, Nike SB, to accompany a traveling exhibition, the collection includes four extremely limited-edition Dunks that are now worth several tens of thousands of dollars. From top to bottom: Nike SB Dunk Low Paris (2002), London (2004), Tokyo (2004), and NYC Pigeon (2005).

Believe Hype:

the

Sneakers Go Big

At the dawn of the year 2000, the rules of the game changed for brands, who were fully aware that sneakers appealed to consumers more for their design than for their performance. A lifestyle customer base and community of collectors developed, driving brands to refocus their strategies on rereleasing retro models and producing limited editions. It was the era of collaborations, campouts, the Internet, social media, and hype—that unique energy that has guided brands ever since.

The emergence of the lifestyle market challenged the existing strategies of most sportswear brands. Now, aesthetics trumped performance in a quest to produce innovative products for a new clientele. Limited editions and exclusive releases were the name of the game.

Brands were now aware that the lifestyle market had overtaken sports, so they slowed production of new pairs in favor of rereleasing retro models, revisiting historically popular designs with different colorways and materials. At the same time, they invested in the production of limited editions to satisfy a growing number of collectors. These sneakers, released in small—even miniscule—quantities, were intended to create a buzz among sneakerheads. This took different forms. For example, regional exclusives were only released in one part of

The Hunt for the
Limited
Edit

the world or a single country in response to local demand for a specific model. A sneaker might also be reserved for a single retail outlet or designed for a specific event, like Halloween, Valentine's Day, or Lunar New Year, and produced in related colorways. Every occasion was now an opportunity to create a unique pair of sneakers.

The most original designs, however, came out of collaborations. To brands, the concept was the ideal way to attract consumers hungry for exclusivity. Manufacturers invited partners to contribute to a creative vision for a given model. A series of successful collabs in the 1990s—Jil Sander × Puma, Nike × Wu-Tang Clan, Nike × Junya Watanabe—triggered an avalanche in 2002: as Adidas launched its collaborative line Y-3 with designer Yohji Yamamoto, Nike began its HTM program in partnership with designer Hiroshi Fujiwara, and long-term collaborations with the Atmos boutique and the Supreme brand, through its new Skateboarding (SB) division.

The new millennium marked a turning point in the sneaker industry. Everything depends on context and this one was favorable: broadband had arrived in most homes, sparking a revolution that enabled anyone to access any information they wanted, about any given subject, in a matter of clicks. The passion for sneakers developed and took shape via the Internet as the first blogs and forums appeared. A community was created, sharing knowledge and news about new releases. And the releases just kept coming.

Nike SB alone consolidated the new dynamics at work. In addition to designing visionary limited-edition collaborations and colorways, Nike's SB division chose to limit distribution to selected independent skate shops when it was launched in 2002. The decision was a response to consumer desire for authenticity, which illustrates retail's evolution toward more exclusive offers. Until this point, brands could sell their products in big-box stores, but now they reduced the number of retail outlets and developed new ones in the form of pop-up stores, invitation-only events, and customizing services like the original Nike iD (now Nike By You). The era of all-exclusive and limited-edition sneakers had arrived.

on

Guess What ? "We work really, really hard to make everything seem effortless," said James Jebbia in *032c* magazine, describing how his brand, Supreme, operates. The New York brand didn't want to overdo things or find itself with unsold product on its hands, so from its very beginnings in 1994 it decided to sell its products in small quantities through weekly drops. This decision had an entirely different effect: each of Supreme's creations, stamped with its signature box logo, became a collector's item. Supreme came to symbolize streetwear hype—culminating in a collab with Louis Vuitton in 2017—and the success of limited editions. The brand is a textbook case and major inspiration for footwear companies.

Facing page
Released in 2020, the Union LA × Air Jordan 4 Off Noir, the second project between the Los Angeles store Union and Jordan Brand, is a coveted collab.

Above, top
Nicknamed "Habibi," this Nike SB Dunk resulted from a collaboration between the Swoosh and Frame, a skate shop in Dubai. Released in December 2020, on the UAE National Day, the pair commands high prices on the resale market.

Above, bottom
The Nike Dunk Low and High Black and White are both ever-popular basics.

Colla
Co
Colla

Chosen by brands as the best way to drum up interest in their sneakers, collaborations have become increasingly high profile. In fact, they form one of the keystones of the market as we know it.

While Chuck Taylor's involvement with Converse in the 1930s was very much a collaboration, as was Stan Smith's with Adidas and Jordan's with Nike, the collaboration as we know it today appeared in the late 1990s. In response to consumers' voracious appetite for unique products, collaborations satisfied sneakerheads by offering unique designs and original stories through exclusive releases.

Collaboration covered a broad spectrum of partnerships. There were retailers with natural ties to the manufacturers whose products they sold, thrown in with a random mix of

sportswear giants like Foot Locker, concept stores like Colette in Paris, and small skate shops. Then came major figures in street culture, those who had worn the sneaker as a symbol of rebellion: first, rappers became tastemakers, long after the hit release Run-DMC × Adidas in 1986; then artists claimed the sneaker as work of art in 2003, when Nike launched its Artist Series; and streetwear brands like Bape, Stüssy, Palace, and, of course, Supreme, made the sneaker a style must-have. Finally, there were the luxury houses and designers; having long rejected the idea of moving into the realm of sports, they finally offered their own vision of the sneaker and teamed up with historic brands.

Regardless of the partnership, collaboration is a win-win. Manufacturers attract their partners' market, while their partner reaches sneakerheads. In the quest for new consumers, the brand kills two birds with one stone: the collab sneaker is labeled as exceptional, a rarity the brand can capitalize on. As sneakers went mainstream and social media intensified, the various participants continued to cultivate the imbalance between supply and demand, increasing their appeal. The collab became the perfect tool to drive a sales strategy based on exclusivity and the best way to generate hype: the term is now synonymous with cool—whether it be a product, a brand, or a designer—and the associated process, set in motion by media buzz, that triggers intense enthusiasm and compulsive consumption.

b!
lab!
b!

How has the market evolved from occasional collabs to a collab-driven market in twenty years? How have yesterday's barriers broken down to the point that sportswear giants now partner with leaders in other sectors, like Nike × Louis Vuitton or Adidas × Gucci? It's all a matter of milestones—events that made sneakers a global phenomenon, each involving a collaboration.

Guess What ? Today, collaboration is a vital strand of the sneaker industry and unites participants in the creative process, but for decades it was considered anathema. Dapper Dan is a perfect illustration of how much things have changed. In the 1980s, this Harlem-based designer recontextualized luxury brand logos by placing them on clothes and sneakers. Taken to court for counterfeiting, he was obliged to close his store, which had been popular with rappers and athletes. But he had the last laugh: his streetwear is now a source of inspiration for luxury brands, and Dapper Dan collaborated with Gucci in 2017. As for his Air Force 1s emblazoned with the Louis Vuitton monogram, immortalized on several rap CD jackets in the 1980s, they found an echo in a collab between Nike and the French fashion house in 2022. Proof that today, anything is possible.

Facing page
Gucci unveiled a new collaboration with Adidas for its Fall/Winter 2022–23 collection "Exquisite," presented at Milan Fashion Week.

Left
Released in 2022, the Louis Vuitton × Nike Air Force 1 was created by designer Virgil Abloh in tribute to hip-hop culture and, more specifically, to the bootlegs of the movement's early days.

Unforg

Collab

There have been hundreds of sneaker collaborations, from one-offs to long-term partnerships. Here are some of the biggest hits that have shaped the market.

1996
Vans × Supreme

The streetwear brand Supreme, which would become one of the most popular collaborators in the industry, made its first foray into footwear with Vans.

1984
Nike × The Three Amigos

Three stores in Baltimore encouraged Nike to ship them pairs of the discontinued Air Force 1. It was the first collaboration between a manufacturer and a retailer, and the first limited-edition sneaker.

ettable

orations

1998

Puma × Jil Sander

The first collaboration between a manufacturer and a luxury brand included sneakers and a clothing line.

1999

Nike × Wu-Tang Clan

Nike's first encounter with rap produced this Dunk emblazoned with the logo of New York's Wu-Tang Clan. Released as an ultra-limited Friends & Family edition, it immediately became a collector's item.

Nike × Comme des Garçons

Nike's high-fashion collaborations began with Japanese designer Junya Watanabe of label Comme des Garçons.

2000

Nike × Stüssy

The Swoosh introduced its long-term collaboration with California streetwear brand Stüssy by revisiting the Huarache model.

2002

Adidas × Yohji Yamamoto

The lasting success of this first collaborative line between a manufacturer and a luxury brand laid the foundation for high fashion's partnership with sportswear.

Nike × Atmos

Nike reserved its first ever Air Max collaboration for the Tokyo shop, whose safari-print AM1 became a classic.

2003

Nike Artists Series

Nike launched a program inviting graffiti artists to revisit classic releases. Futura and Stash were the first to delight collectors with particularly original Dunk and Air Force 1 designs.

Nike SB × Supreme

Nike's skate division dropped a Dunk pack in collaboration with Supreme, featuring the cement print from the Air Jordan 3. It was the division's first hit and a must-have for collectors.

Nike HTM

This R&D group named for the initials of its creators— Fragment founder Hiroshi Fujiwara, Nike designer Tinker Hatfield, and Nike CEO Mark Parker—redrew the limits of design through experimentation.

Adidas × Bape

Another major collaboration with a streetwear brand, this one was initiated by Adidas. Japanese brand Bape designed limited-edition packs of the Superstar and Superskate.

Reebok × Jay-Z

The S. Carter designed by Jay-Z and Reebok was the first signature shoe by a rapper to be a hit.

2004

Adidas × Stella McCartney

The three-stripe brand confirmed its status as leader in the high-fashion collab market when it signed a long-term partnership with Stella McCartney, the first well-known designer to create a sportswear line for women.

2005

Jordan × Undefeated

The first collab for the Jordan line was carried out in partnership with the Los Angeles retailer Undefeated and produced an Air Jordan 4 inspired by US Army flight jackets. Only seventy-two pairs were released, making them highly sought after.

Nike SB × Jeff Staple

See p. 102

2006

Adidas × Jeremy Scott

Adidas made another foray into fashion in 2006 with designer Jeremy Scott, who is remembered for his extravagant creations that embodied the playful fashion of the time.

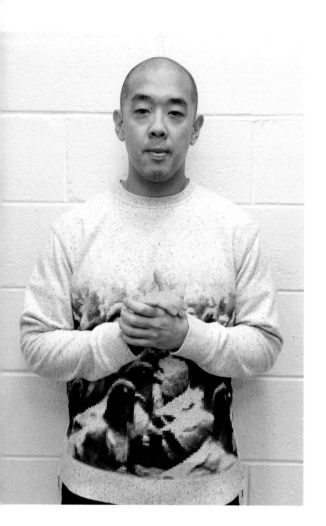

This is what really triggered sneaker madness. The 2005 release of the Jeff Staple × Nike SB Dunk Low Pigeon brought sneakers, until then the preserve of those in the know, into the spotlight. And for good reason: it was an extraordinary drop.

In 2003, Nike's freshly minted skateboard division distinguished itself through a brilliant creative approach. To accompany the traveling exhibition *White Dunk: Evolution of an Icon*—which featured specially commissioned works based on the Dunk model by twenty-five Japanese artists—Nike SB decided to produce extremely limited editions of pairs created for each host city. The Paris, Tokyo, London, and New York City Dunks were released between 2003 and 2005, and form a now-legendary City Pack. And the NYC Dunk is a legend in its own right.

For the New York version, the Nike SB teams collaborated with designer Jeff Staple, who wanted to create a sneaker that represented his city. He chose the pigeon as the signature logo and a colorway inspired by the bird's plumage. Only one hundred and fifty pairs were made, and they were distributed to a few skate shops in the Big Apple. Staple reserved thirty for his boutique, Reed Space, on the Lower East Side. Unlike the others, these pairs were all numbered—a detail that made all the difference to sneakerheads.

Jeff Sta
× Nike SB Dunk Pigeon: The Original Disrupter

Some lined up outside the store four days before the release, waiting patiently in the February cold and sleeping in tents.

On the big day, chaos reigned. More than one hundred and fifty people jostled for the sneaker grail. There were reports of people being mugged for their purchases, and the police were called to restore order and to escort the lucky new owners safely from the premises. Knives, machetes, and baseball bats were found in the area after the crowd had dispersed. The day after the release, February 23, 2005, the New York Post featured the event as front-page news under the headline "Sneak Attack." This unprecedented attention from print and television media brought sneaker culture out into the open. Nike was taken completely unawares, but if the company had been worried about bad press, it wasn't for long.

Sneaker media described the Pigeon's release as a turning point that catapulted sneaker mania into the mainstream. In addition to enlarging the fanbase, the model sent the message that sneakers could make money—pairs were selling on eBay for $1,000 the day they were released. Campouts became common, as did resales and counterfeits. The market effects were compelling as well. Barriers that had once seemed impenetrable began to break down, and sneakers started to attract new artists, celebrities, and brands. Above all, the Pigeon intensified the pursuit of the limited edition, with brands hoping to reproduce what it had generated: hype.

Facing page
Portrait of Jeff Staple, 2014. After working on the Nike SB Dunk Pigeon, the designer collaborated with a number of other brands like Puma, Crocs, Bellroy, Octopus, Fossil, and Tumi.

Above
The iconic Nike SB Dunk Pigeon. According to Jeff Staple, the pigeon perfectly embodies New York street mentality—the animal has managed to adapt and thrive in a hostile urban environment.

ple

Guess What ? The day after the Pigeon Dunk was released, a representative of the Timberland brand came into Jeff Staple's store and said, "We want a riot, too!" The company was already eager to discuss a collaboration—a perfect illustration of the repercussions this sneaker would have on the industry and on brand strategy.

2007

Bape × Kanye West

Kanye West's first official collab was a memorable one: a Bape Sta in a colorway based on the design of his first album, *The College Dropout*.

2008

Nike 1World

With the 1World Program, Nike continued its artistic partnerships and invited a dozen artists, musicians, and other personalities to revisit the Air Force 1. Versions by KAWS, Clot, Michael Lau, and Booba became classics.

2009

Louis Vuitton × Kanye West

See p. 106

Nike × Kanye West

See p. 106

Nike × Patta

The first collab between Nike and the Dutch store produced an Air Max 1 pack celebrating the sneaker's fifth anniversary. The cherry on the cake was a collector trio designed by Dutch artist Parra.

2012

Nike × Tom Sachs

This pair may not look like much, but its conception is what makes the difference: artist Tom Sachs used materials developed by NASA to provide maximum resistance to the elements— another way to attract collectors.

2013

Adidas × Raf Simons

Ever on the cutting edge of fashion, Adidas teamed up with the Belgian designer and later creative director for Dior. The collab produced an instant hit, the Ozweego, that heralded the arrival of the dad shoe trend.

2015

Yeezy

Kanye West's collaborative line with Adidas, announced in 2013, took shape with this first model, the Adidas Yeezy Boost 750.

Kanye West: The Revolutionary

Kanye West's sneaker revolution began in 2009. The rapper changed the face of the industry by generating remarkable hype for his avant-garde designs and through his novel approach to marketing.

West, now known as Ye, neither invented the concept of luxury sneakers nor inaugurated collabs with hip-hop artists. But he pushed the envelope with his phenomenally successful products, foremost through design: as a rapper, he samples loops from obscure archives; as a designer, West draws on multiple references to create futurist forms like the Nike Air Yeezy 1 and 2, considered the perfect fusion of sports and lifestyle. His alluring, radical aesthetic is backed up by his own personality: Ye is a hitmaker who knows how to use his popularity to promote his products. An expert at organizing happenings, he heightens interest for his designs by posting slick teasers on social media. Throw in a strategy of ultra-limited editions and it's clear that West's approach is the very definition of hype.

The rapper's creations broke down barriers and attracted a mainstream audience to rap and hip-hop subcultures. Conversely, young hip-hop fans took an interest in luxury when the artist collaborated with Louis Vuitton. Campouts leading up to sneaker releases took on titanic proportions: lines formed outside stores up to a month and a half before the release of an Air Yeezy 2! Resale prices reached levels never before seen or even imagined. The first Air Yeezy 2s appeared on the resale market priced at over $3,000, and at $4,000 for the last version, the Red October, released after West's official departure for Adidas. Nike took note of the figures and decided to release its most anticipated new products online rather than in stores.

When it comes to West, forget categories and labels. He has always insisted that he's more than a musician and describes himself as a creator in the broadest sense of the word, which he has demonstrated in the realms of fashion and sneakers. West began seriously designing around the time he released his first opus, *The College Dropout*, before signing his first official collab with Bape in 2007. He really pushed the boundaries two years later, when he teamed up with Louis Vuitton for a footwear collection and by signing a contract with Nike, which made him the first non-athlete to be given a sneaker partnership.

Ultimately, West began shaping the current market as soon as he teamed up with Nike: he confirmed the sneaker's status as fashion accessory, paved the way for previously unimaginable collaborations, instituted social media as a primary marketing tool, encouraged the systematic use of raffles for limited editions, and boosted the resale market. He continued to exert his influence on the industry with his successful Yeezy line, produced with Adidas, and his impact can also be gauged through the rise of those who have followed in his footsteps to reach peak hype: Virgil Abloh and Travis Scott were among his protégés. It remains to be seen if Ye will continue to shape the industry that he helped to build, in the light of his terminated contract with the Three Stripes in 2022, and the fact that brands and celebrities have turned their back on him, after his numerous controversial comments.

Facing page

The new Kanye West, now known as Ye, frequently goes out with his face completely masked.

Above

A "Pop × Culture" sale held by the British auction house Bonhams in 2020. In the foreground, a pair of Nike Air Yeezy 2 Red Octobers.

Right

Already a classic, the Yeezy Boost 700 Wave Runner is one of the brand's most sought-after models. Following its release in 2017, Adidas restocked several times to satisfy consumers' insatiable demand.

Guess What ? The pair of Nike Air Yeezy 1s worn by Kanye West during the 2008 Grammy Awards ceremony sold at auction in April 2021 for the heady sum of $1.8 million. The sample sneakers had given a preview of his first collab with Nike, released a year later in stores, which generated enormous anticipation. This pair of Nike Air Yeezy 1s became the most expensive sneaker in history—triple the previous record. It was surpassed in 2023 by a pair of Air Jordan 13s worn by Michael Jordan.

2017

Adidas × Pharrell Williams × Chanel

A regular collaborator with Adidas, Pharrell Williams briefly revived the hype around the NMD with a trio that included Chanel. This was the luxury brand's first footwear collab. Only five hundred pairs were produced, and they were sold exclusively at the concept store Colette in Paris.

Nike × Off-White

"AIR"

See p. 114

Jordan × Colette

2017

When Colette announced that it was closing for good, the Jordan Brand designed this sneaker to celebrate the Paris concept store's twenty years in business.

Nike × Travis Scott

See p. 116

2018

Nike × Sean Wotherspoon

The owner of a fashionable vintage boutique in the US, Sean Wotherspoon won a design contest organized by Nike with this hybrid sneaker that combined the Air Max 1 and 97. Its pop colors and corduroy upper made a splash and ushered him into the sneakerverse to great acclaim.

Nike × Fear of God

In 2018, Nike teamed up with Jerry Lorenzo's chic streetwear label to produce this hit. The partnership resulted in several luxury sneakers, including a highly collectible Air FOG 1.

2019

New Balance × Aimé Leon Dore

New Balance's recent comeback was due in part to its visionary collaborations. This noteworthy partnership with New York brand Aimé Leon Dore modernized several retro silhouettes with new aesthetics.

Nike × Sacai

Nike's partnership with the Japanese high-fashion brand began in 2015, but entered history in 2018. The hybrid LDWaffle, revealed on the runway, generated enormous enthusiasm for its "double-stacked" design.

2020

Jordan × Dior

This is the most iconic sneaker of all time adorned with the monogram of the most prestigious fashion house. The sneaker collab reached its apogee in 2020 with these Air Jordan 1 High and Low, which retailed for the equivalent of about $2,000.

Adidas × Prada

Released at the same time as the Jordan × Dior collab, the Adidas × Prada collab adopted the same winning formula.

New Balance × Casablanca

NB jumped on the high-fashion collab trend by working with Charaf Tajer's young French-Moroccan brand to create sunny, retro-futurist designs.

2022

Nike × Louis Vuitton

The last footwear collab designed by Virgil Abloh, L.V.'s creative director, paid tribute to Dapper Dan's 1980s bootlegs. These Air Force 1s were sold exclusively at auction.

Adidas × Gucci

Adidas responded to prestige with prestige: the three-stripe brand turned to Italy and caused a sensation by joining forces with Gucci.

Adidas × Balenciaga

Another surprise from Adidas in 2022: the brand teamed up with the current high-fashion favorite, Balenciaga. A large clothing collection as well as the Triple S and Stan Smith were released, perpetuating the frantic pursuit of high-fashion collabs.

Architect, Kanye West's right-hand man, DJ, founder of Off-White, artistic director of Louis Vuitton: Virgil Abloh wore as many hats as he had successes. As a footwear designer, he left his indelible mark on recent sneaker history.

Judging by Virgil Abloh's trajectory, the American Dream isn't an illusion after all. The son of immigrants from Ghana, this native of Rockford, Illinois, who "just wanted to find a well-paid job," worked his way up to be artistic director of Louis Vuitton's menswear collections. He wasn't destined for the role: a trained architect, he came to design through his passion for music and fashion.

Virgil Ab
The Hypebeast

Above
Portrait of Virgil Abloh, 2017.

Left
The Louis Vuitton Homme Spring/Summer 2019 fashion show. Virgil Abloh chose the Palais-Royal in Paris as the backdrop for his first collection at the head of the French brand's menswear collections.

Facing page
Virgil Abloh working on the collection The Ten, 2017. The designer revisited ten iconic Nike models, which were instant hits.

loh:

A DJ and fashion designer in his spare time, Abloh met Kanye West in the early 2000s and began working with him. The two men completed a formative internship at Fendi. Then Abloh abandoned architecture to open the concept store RSVP Gallery, in Chicago, which was immediately popular with the in-crowd. He had a radical career shift in 2011, when he was nominated for a Grammy for his work as artistic director of a collaborative album between Kanye West and Jay-Z, *Watch the Throne*.

The following year, Abloh made a sensational entry into fashion. His label Pyrex Vision only lasted for one collection, but it was successful enough to launch his career. In 2013, Pyrex, the "artistic project," gave way to Off-White, a "serious approach to fashion" that confirmed his status as a designer. With oversize cuts, huge logos, and XXL prints, Off-White disrupted the codes of luxury and embodied the streetwear wave overtaking the runways. A finalist for the prestigious LVMH prize in 2015, Abloh saw his popularity increase, paving the way for collaborations.

In 2017, Nike asked him to reimagine ten iconic silhouettes for The Ten collection, which featured unique designs that sparked a frenzy of interest. Like his associate Kanye West before him, Abloh was successful in stoking interest in his sneakers, including for resale, creating the ultimate hype. Basking in public acclaim, a year later he signed with Louis Vuitton and initiated a series of collabs with a variety of brands including Ikea, Evian, and Baccarat. His success story came to a tragic end in 2021 when he passed away following a battle with cancer. But Abloh, creator of possibilities, left a lasting impression on the fashion and sneaker industries.

Virgil Abloh's sneakers have unique, recognizable features like quotes, a zip tie on the laces, and industrial text on the mid-section. For the rest, Abloh applied his "3 percent rule": he only modified 3 percent of a sneaker's existing design so that it would remain identifiable.

Kanye West, Virgil Abloh—and Travis Scott. The rapper from Houston followed in the wake of his illustrious predecessors to become the new embodiment of hype on Planet Sneaker, pushing the limits that they had previously redefined.

The year 2017 was a pivotal one: the Supreme × Louis Vuitton collaboration was released and Abloh delivered his The Ten collection with Nike. The same year, Nike introduced another collaborator who would boost the brand's influence in footwear: Travis Scott. The Texan artist nicknamed "La Flame" was rap's rising star. His first two albums were successful and gallons of ink were spilled on his live performances. His future was looking

Travis Scott:
The New King

bright, and his newly minted relationship with Kylie Jenner made him a media sensation. Nike picked up the sweet scent of success at the right moment.

Scott's widely acclaimed album *Astroworld*, released in August 2018, made him an international superstar. After demonstrating his playful, psychedelic touch on the design of an Air Force 1 that featured reflective, repositionable details bearing his Cactus Jack signature, La Flame was welcomed with open arms at Nike. A series of projects was initiated to revisit great classics, notably the Jordan line, from the 4 to the 6, and the Air Jordan 1. For the latter, Scott flipped the central Swoosh logo to create another personal stamp. The models all sold out and resold for sky-high prices.

Using methods proven by his mentor Kanye West, especially teasers on social media, Scott became Nike's preferred vehicle for revisiting retro models like the Dunk, which he rejuvenated with the release of his own version in 2020. The year was a turning point

Above
The Travis Scott × Air Jordan High Military Blue and its inverted Swoosh, the Texan rapper's signature.

Facing page
La Flame on the sidelines of the fashion show presenting "Cactus Jack Dior" for the Dior Summer 2022 men's collection.

for the rapper. Besides Nike, leaders in other sectors began to approach him for partnerships: Epic Games for virtual concerts on Fortnite, Playstation and McDonald's for merch, and Dior for its campaign with Jordan Brand, which was extended for an extra year with a collection that included clothing and accessories.

Whether partnering with a sportswear manufacturer, fast-food chain, or luxury brand, Scott managed to move through very different spheres while staying true to his image. Everything he touched turned to gold, it seemed. However, his rise to the top was brutally interrupted one night in November 2021, when ten people died in a stampede during a festival he had organized. Sued for negligence and abandoned by several sponsors, the King of Hype toppled from his pedestal. But not for long: he quickly returned to the limelight, buoyed by Nike's continued partnership.

Left, top
On April 23, 2020, during the Covid-19 lockdown, Travis Scott gave a historic concert—in the online game Fortnite.

Left, bottom
Travis Scott performing at the 2016 Made in America Festival in Philadelphia.

Above
The first Astroworld Festival, organized by Travis Scott in 2018.

Below
Travis Scott outside a McDonald's in Downey, California, 2020. The rapper created a sensation by presenting the first merch collaboration with the famous fast-food chain.

Guess What ?

Travis Scott earned a $10 million annual salary from his contract with Nike in 2020, according to *Forbes*. The business magazine points out that this is only 10 percent of what he earned from his creative partnerships in that year alone, and that he is actually worth much more. The publication argues that the popularity of his sneakers has made him a tastemaker, leading to more collaborations and, more significantly, giving him "the standing to change the rules of celebrity sponsorships." For while celebrities usually do what brands tell them to, the rapper dictates his own rules. So, for his sneakers with Nike, "not so much as an eyelet gets altered without his approval."

The Digital World:

Sneakers' cult following has kept pace with the growth of online culture. Brands have capitalized on the new El Dorado to sell even more products, using the Internet to serve more effectively than ever their strategy of producing limited editions.

The Internet has changed everything, in every sector, and the sneaker industry is no exception. The Worldwide Web has become a marketing arena that sportswear brands use to multiply their retail outlets and promote their products. And while they may have looked unfavorably on the first blogs and forums that shared information about their releases—like when Nike attacked the sneakerhead hub Nike Talk—they have changed their tune over time and with the

emergence of an interactive Web culture. In the 2010s, social networks mushroomed. More than forums and specialized sites, these online communities for sharing encouraged the democratization of sneakers and united fans. Brands inundated these spaces and established new marketing approaches, increasing the power of the existing limited-edition strategy.

A Strategic Ideal

The most influential collaborators, such as Kanye West and Travis Scott, have wholeheartedly adopted these tactics. Both use social media, especially Instagram, to reveal their creations long before they are released—sometimes more than a year ahead—with teasers offering previews of specific designs. This approach benefits brands in two ways: it provides wide-reaching communication with little investment and

raises fans' expectations ahead of time. While international superstars have the strongest influence, other participants in the ecosystem have been chosen to convey messaging, from influencers to leakers—sneaker accounts specialized in leaking previews of unreleased shoes. This gives rise to the powerful desire that is characteristic of hype on social media, well before the sneakers' release, which also takes place online.

Campouts were too disruptive, so brands and stores abandoned the physical in favor of the digital by organizing drops on a first-come-first-served basis and, for more limited models, adopting a raffle system. Was this a simple security measure? Not exactly: these marketing methods fit perfectly into brand strategy. In addition to naturally increasing demand, drops and raffles make it easier to control distribution and, once again, to create buzz. The day of an important release, the hashtag Nike or Yeezy Adidas is always trending on Twitter—a reflection of consumer sentiment that also provides a surfeit of marketing for the brand in question.

A digital strategy doesn't stop at the release of a popular collaboration—it's just another starting point. Manufacturers redirect disappointed buyers who were unable to cop a release toward their catalog, even suggesting alternatives produced in greater quantities. Travis Scott's ultra-limited Air Jordan 1 High, for example, was followed by a Dark Mocha version in a largely similar colorway that met with equal success. New Balance follows a similar strategy: the 550s cosigned by the fashionable label Aimé Leon Dore are always followed by a range of similar colorways. This rounds everything off nicely, although, at the end of the day, the consumer is often left feeling frustrated. But then, isn't that the point?

Facing page
Travis Scott wearing pieces from his collaboration with Jordan Brand.

Top, right
Everything Travis Scott and Kylie Jenner wear when they make an appearance—especially on Instagram—becomes a hit. Here, they are pictured with their daughter, Stormi.

Guess What? In early 2020, Travis Scott's partner, Kylie Jenner, posed on Instagram, in front of her three hundred million followers, wearing several limited-edition SB Dunks. The effect was immediate: in the days following her posts, the number of transactions on the resale platform StockX doubled, even quadrupled, and the models she wore, which were already rare and expensive, skyrocketed 30 to 50 percent in value. More recently, her sister Kim Kardashian donned a pair of pink Air Max 95s, triggering a 2,400 percent increase in searches for the product on specialized sites. These figures highlight the power of social media, influencers, and celebrities, and clearly show how worthwhile it is for brands to work with them.

A Guide to
Ra

The Air Jordan 1 Retro High OG x Off-White is yours. Share your latest pick up with your friends.

GOT 'EM

SHARE

Because brands now favor digital over physical retail outlets for their most anticipated releases, they use raffles to give potential purchasers the opportunity to buy their products. Here's how this frustrating system works.

Raffles are not new to the sneakerverse. Brands used them in the analog past, like when Nike SB organized sweepstakes in the early 2000s to distribute most of the models in the City Pack. Brands and stores resorted to this method to avoid the chaotic lines that formed when demand outstripped supply for certain drops, such as the final model in the City Pack—the SB Dunk Pigeon—or Kanye West's creations. The system was initially offered in stores, before moving online, where it fit perfectly into marketing and communication strategies.

A raffle is a random draw that gives fans the chance to buy a sneaker—but winning the right to purchase is a concept that many find infuriating. All distributors use the system, brands and retailers alike. Methods vary depending on the type of raffle. Participants register for online raffles via a form that includes contact information and payment method, and is accessible for a few days

Left
Every participant in a Nike SNKRS app raffle hopes to receive this message.

ffles

before the official release date. On smartphone apps like Nike's SNKRS and Adidas's Confirmed, participants must create an account beforehand and register at a predetermined time. Finally, on Instagram, registration is confirmed in exchange for an action required by the raffle host—participants must add a follow, create a story, leave a comment, etc. The results are announced in the days—or minutes in the case of apps—following the raffle.

Few people like raffles: quantities are far lower than the number of participants and there is little chance of winning, especially since the system is plagued by bots. These paying computer programs are developed to increase the chances of winning a raffle, and they completely automate entries. Bots are particularly effective for "first come, first served" drops, where they can clean out inventory in a matter of seconds by multiplying orders without drawing the attention of website security. But they are also used to accumulate entries during raffles. Resellers, who intend to resell sneakers for a profit, are the primary users.

Suffice it to say, raffles do more to generate disappointment than they do to democratize access to sneakers, which online releases, with their lack of geographic barriers, were supposed to do. Brands are trying to curb the use of bots by strengthening security and developing new formats for drops. Nike has even begun to reward the most committed users of its SNKRS app by offering them exclusive access to buy sneakers ahead of official releases. However, brands are not about to abandon raffles, the culmination of

a strategy of scarcity that increases the value of their products and the brand's own attractiveness. It's just too bad for consumers. If they really want access to a sneaker, they're often forced to turn to the resale market.

Five million people signed up for a raffle organized by Dior to sell some eight thousand pairs of its Air Jordan 1 High and Low collab sneakers. The Parisian fashion brand reports that this outrageous number of participants—equal to the population of Ireland—applied online during a period of just nine hours. A perfect illustration of the hype around these two ultra-limited-edition sneakers, which sold for the equivalent of about $2,000.

"Sneaker
hype
is clearly on

Yeezy Mafia, sneaker leakers par excellence

Created in 2016, the collective Yeezy Mafia has had a significant influence on sneaker culture. By leaking information about yet-to-be-released models, the platform has established itself as the largest media outlet dedicated to the Yeezy label and cultivates hype around it. We met with the founder of this nebulous entity, which now has more than four million followers.

Yeezy Mafia has been described as many things: media platform, influencer, reseller, and brand. Can you give us an overview of its trajectory and tell us where the collective is now?
Yeezy Mafia started out as a private group of resellers. We didn't intend to become a media platform. But, little by little, the network grew. We started having access to information that no one else had, so we shared it on social media and people went wild. From there it snowballed, and we attracted the attention of major American media outlets, brands, and even Ye himself. This has been the case since 2016 now, and the platform has naturally evolved and made several transitions. For example, we are no longer resellers; we've shifted into creative marketing by working with brands.

Yeezy Mafia is a symbol of the enthusiasm for Kanye West's designs. How would you describe his impact on the sneaker industry? Would it be correct to say that he really created the hype around sneakers?
Kanye revolutionized the industry. Before he arrived on the scene, sneakers were still seen as a sports accessory by most people, and an object of desire by a few insiders. He used his artist's touch to make a place for himself through innovative designs, be that with Nike, Louis Vuitton, or Adidas, who he gave a fresh image. Kanye didn't invent hype per se, since there was already incredible hype around certain limited editions. But it only concerned small circles of basketball purists. He created what I would call mainstream hype: his designs brought together music fans, sneaker fans, and fashion fans, regardless of geography, age, or gender. That had never been done before.

"Yeezy Mafia started out as a private group of resellers."

How would you explain hype? What is its scope in the sneaker industry, what does it consist of, and what is the outcome?
Hype is the equation between current trend, supply, and demand. It relates to all products, not only limited editions or collaborations—Kanye, like other influencers, has managed to drum up incredible hype for some really basic pairs. But for a pair to create hype, it has to be treated like a collaboration. Adidas's NMD caused a big stir when it was released because it was well done from a marketing point of view. But the opposite effect is more common. For example,

the decline."

the Yeezy 380 was very popular when it was released in its original version, but was closely followed by another, less effective and poorly marketed colorway, which had a negative impact on the model's popularity. Hype is a holistic process and it takes a lot of work to maintain it. That's the problem with brands: they tend to slow their efforts after a success by getting ahead of themselves. We're working on this aspect now, by advising sportswear manufacturers so they are able to keep up the hype over the long term.

Many successful release stories include mention of the manufacturer's surprise, of being caught off guard by the level of enthusiasm for their products. Is it true to say that they created hype in the sneaker industry, or did they just maintain it after it emerged naturally?

Brands are now trying to create hype, but yes, I remember very clearly that the concept was foreign to them when we started in 2016. By leaking information, we were seen as the bad guys who sabotaged marketing plans. Today, leaks are central to

"When we first started, there was a drop every three months. So you had to psych yourself up, get prepared. Now every brand organizes several drops each week."

manufacturers' strategies. I would say that hype really became their driving force in 2019, precisely when sneaker hype started to decline. Brands were asking themselves what they were missing, how they could replicate the formula that had made them successful.

**We still talk about hype, but the industry
seems to have changed since Yeezy Mafia
was created: following Kanye West's example
of promising "Yeezys for everyone," brands
have increased drops, and limited editions
are not as limited as they once were.**

The number of releases is increasing,
while our attention spans are growing shorter
and shorter. When we first started, there was
a drop every three months. So you had to
psych yourself up, get prepared. Now every
brand organizes several drops each week.
The game has changed and I think that the
Covid-19 pandemic dealt a huge blow to
sneaker hype, which I see as being clearly
on the decline. It's a personal observation,
but all the big resellers that I know who
contributed to creating this hype stopped
with the pandemic and went into NFTs. The
purchasing systems have changed and
resale prices have dropped significantly.
I think we're going to reach a point where
everyone will be able to have the pair they
want, and brands will sell all of their product.
That's where we're headed. The sportswear
giants don't receive anything from the resale
market, so when I see that Nike is starting to
wage war on StockX, it tells me something
must be up.

Remark
Re

able

sale

The industry being what it is, it can't—and won't—satisfy the growing number of sneakerheads, so the resale market has become essential. This secondary market, where new pairs of sold-out models sell for sometimes eye-watering prices, has gone from an obscure parallel economy to a multi-million-dollar industry.

Following the widespread popularity of kicks and the limited-edition strategy employed by brands, the resale market has carved out a niche for itself in the sneaker game. But despite recent media attention, the phenomenon is not actually new.

Re

The resale market—which refers to the activity of reselling sneakers after their retail release for profit—exclusively relates to sneakers kept in their original box and in pristine "box-fresh" condition, as opposed to secondhand. Wearing a sneaker devalues it.

At its most basic, a sneaker's value is determined by the law of supply and demand, although other factors do come into play, and some pairs can reach more than a hundred times the original price. Initially focused on limited editions and discontinued retro models, the resale market expanded as sneakers grew in popularity. It has definitely kept pace with the product: as long as sneakers have been desirable, they have been bought with the intention of reselling.

sale:
Threat
or Promise?

The resale market emerged with the modern sneaker craze in the 1980s, the golden era when kicks achieved cult status. At the time, markets were divided up by region and brands constantly sought to create new products. Demand often outstripped supply, and purchase for resale became a feature of the sneaker economy. It mostly concerned collectors, or individuals making transactions through word of mouth and hand to hand. However, stores also began to market sought-after but unavailable sneakers, whether home grown or from abroad. In the mid-1980s, young Europeans traveled to New York and filled their suitcases with models they couldn't find back home, with the aim of selling them for a profit upon their return. Cult boutiques made a name for themselves stocking these lucky finds, to the delight of European hip-hop fans seeking to replicate the style of their idols in the United States.

Left
Sneakers kept in their original box are now true collector's items.

In the following decade, alongside the rise of the lifestyle market, resale grew at a frenzied pace, especially in 1995 when the Air Jordan 11 and Air Max 95 were released—and then the Internet magnified the phenomenon. Sneaker resale moved online, first to eBay, where relics and limited-edition products found an outlet, and then the first specialized sites were created in the early 2000s. Flight Club, the original sneaker consignment store, opened in 2005—the same year the SB Dunk Low Pigeon was released—sowing chaos and broadcasting the message that sneakers could be moneymakers. Other milestones in sneaker culture were accompanied by the emergence of new players: in 2009, as Kanye West was launching his revolution, the first sneaker convention, Sneaker Con, was held in New York. And in 2013, the same year Ye left Nike for Adidas, the site Campless was founded. Three years later, it became StockX, the ultimate market reference.

The year 2017 was pivotal: a collab between Supreme and Louis Vuitton led to widespread recognition of street culture and sneakers, Virgil Abloh released The Ten collection, and Travis Scott arrived on the scene. The number of sneaker fans skyrocketed, as did resale figures, and historic auction records were broken every six months, attracting media attention and fostering the emergence of new retail structures. However, what businesses, which have continued to roll out new products ever since, considered a virtuous circle, certain sneakerheads criticized, protesting that resale would kill sneaker culture. With kicks as popular as they are and brands continuing to cultivate a strategy of product scarcity, the resale market is unavoidable today. But it has always been part of the game and has proven its staying power. Despite a notable slowdown since 2022, the market's best days may still lie ahead.

Guess What ? The sneaker resale market was worth $10 billion in 2021—ten times its worth in 2015. According to the latest forecasts, the market will even reach $30 billion by 2030—a figure to be taken with a pinch of salt, in view of the troubles witnessed in 2023. Galloping inflation and repeated restocking by manufacturers have caused prices to fall considerably, and the resale craze has somewhat subsided. Analysts, however, see this as the normalization rather than collapse of the market.

Left
The Off-White × Nike Dunk Low Lot 23/50: this pair is one of fifty colorways in Virgil Abloh's collection "Dear Summer."

Facing page
The Nike Dunk High Black White—a basic colorway that is still very popular with consumers—has a healthy resale market.

134

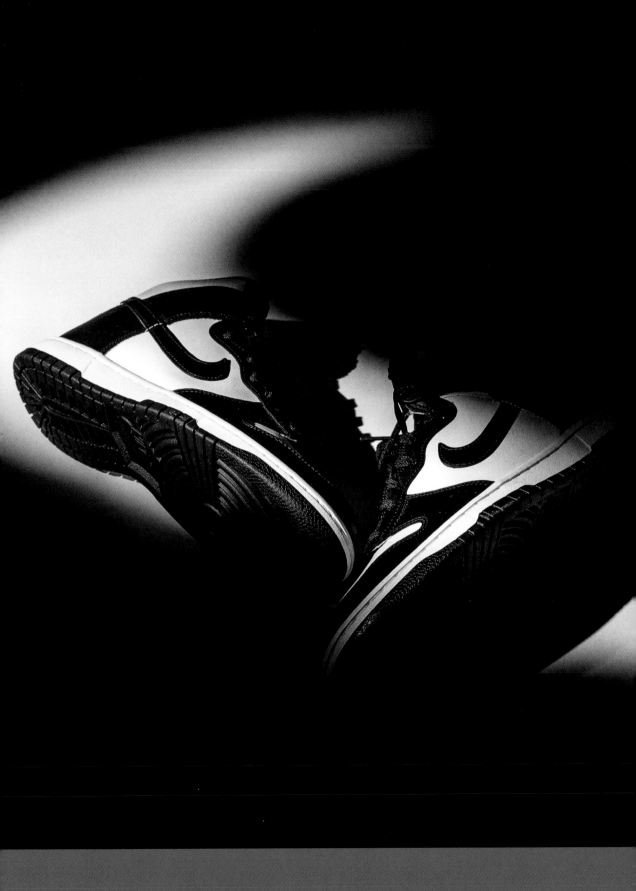

Buying a pair of sneakers for resale is a common practice nowadays. But how is the resale market organized? Let's take a closer look at who makes up the market, how it operates, and the dynamics at work.

For many years, the resale market was a shadowy business, but it soon came out into the open. The process became more accessible and the market was organized around participants and outlets that all promised to deliver new, authentic sneakers: there were events like Sneaker Con, consignment stores such as Flight Club, and specialist platforms like StockX.

The Ins and Outs

Online platforms, by far the most significant in terms of sales volume, may operate differently. For example, the American website StockX puts sellers in touch with buyers, while others respond once an order has been placed, assigning buyers to connect with contacts around the world to find the desired pair.

of the Resa

Market structures depend on individuals, on resellers who range from the high school kid who wants to supplement their allowance to the businessperson who makes a living from it. They're the ones who keep the market alive by getting hold of products. To do this, they go to stores and participate in online drops and raffles. And they'll use any means possible: paying "foot soldiers" to "clean out" a store, or buying bots to net a website's entire stock or multiply the chances of winning a raffle are now commonplace practices. Similarly, with the growing number of resellers attracted by the promise of large profits, "cook groups" have emerged. These subscription-based Discord servers offer information on upcoming drops and advice on how to make the most profit.

Collaborative sneakers are the most coveted by resellers. They command higher prices and bring in more profit, from several hundreds to several thousands of dollars. However, resellers make most of their money from more accessible models that are released more regularly and generate modest margins, in the tens of dollars. This recent evolution is driven by the multiplication of releases and increased stocks, determined by manufacturers in response to the growing popularity of sneakers—and, no doubt, to carve themselves a slice of the resale pie. Since the secondary market remains dependent on the primary one, it evolves according to the strategies of the sportswear giants. As a result, prices tend to be less spectacular than in the past, but the resale

le Market

market is adapting to encompass an ever-increasing range of products. Even a permanent model as basic as the Air Force 1 Low Triple White can be a moneymaker if Nike is slow to restock its website inventory.

Brands themselves have, in fact, long looked favorably on the phenomenon—it is the culmination of their limited-edition strategy: a product's increased value reflects back on the brand's image, furthering its influence and strengthening its appeal.

The resale market also provides brands with additional publicity at no extra cost, and resale data is useful to them: the founder of StockX, which keeps track of all transactions and fluctuations, said that manufacturers were using the site's data to make decisions about future models. Nike and Adidas have even collaborated with the platform on exclusive releases. So, while relations may have grown strained in 2023—judging by manufacturers' efforts to recapture market share, and the increased distrust of Nike, which attacked its former partner head-on and filed several lawsuits—resale still has cred.

Guess What ? Despite more formalization in recent years, the resale market still has some gray zones and is fraught with questionable practices. In 2021, Bloomberg reported on the lucrative activity of a nineteen-year-old reseller who turned out to be the offspring of Ann Hebert, vice-president of Nike North America. Readers were scandalized—and inclined to suspect that the Swoosh executive had granted her son special favors. Hebert eventually resigned, and Nike apologized for putting consumer trust in jeopardy, promising a more relentless fight against bots. And it followed through, even modifying its terms and conditions of sale to this effect!

Resellers

Specialist Platforms
GOAT
Klekt
Stadium Goods
StockX
Wethenew

General Platforms
Depop
eBay
Grailed
Vestiaire Collective
Vinted

Consignment Stores
Afterdrop, Paris
Flight Club, New York, Los Angeles, and Miami
Larry Deadstock, Paris
Skit, Tokyo
Sole Stage, New York and Los Angeles
Urban Necessities, Las Vegas

Events
Crepe City, London
ComplexCon, Long Beach
Sneaker Con, worldwide
Sneakers Event, Paris
Sneakerness, Europe
Sneaker Expo, Los Angeles

Sneakers and the Resale Market: The Right Price

"What are they worth?"
Sneakerheads are obsessed
with this question, which lies
at the heart of the lucrative
resale business. But what
determines the price? Who
defines it? The answer is a
combination of economic
principles, business strategies,
and social media influence.

The resale market is based on the law of supply and demand, and sneaker prices also depend on this age-old economic principle. Simply put, the more rare and coveted a model, the higher its value. At work are several factors, such as the popularity of the person asked to collaborate, the quantity produced, and how the sneaker is commercialized. And because this information is generally known in advance of a release, resellers already have an idea of their future asking price. Interactions on social media are another indicator of desirability that they can work from. However, for a clear answer, they'll wait for StockX.

222€   507€ 488€   625€   472€   715€

2021

2020

970€ 1229€   1067€ 286€   320€   163€

2016

2021

The Union × Nike Dunk Low Argon, from the recent Passport Pack designed by the Swoosh with the California retailer.

Right
These Nike Dunk Low and Adidas NMD illustrate the volatility of prices. While one soared after a period of decline, the other got off to a successful start, then abruptly plummeted.

This resale leader acts as a price guide for the market, much like the automobile industry's Kelley Blue Book indicates the values of used and new vehicles. It lists bids and offers, and establishes a benchmark price that everyone in the market uses as a reference. Sometimes, however, a reseller might set their own price: in this case, they would have acquired most or all of a release, or stock-piled a product and waited—months, maybe even years—for it to become rare. This can create unexpected fluctuations. Like

stocks, sneaker prices aren't fixed, and they can skyrocket or plummet, depending on a number of factors.

Brands are the first to influence the value of their products at resale. A first-class collab will have a positive effect on the model in question. For example, the Dunk, which went more or less unnoticed before 2019, became one of Nike's bestsellers after several successful collaborations that generated hype and, by extension, increased the

popularity of all listed versions of the model. Abundance, on the other hand, can have the opposite effect. If a brand releases too many different colorways in too short a period of time, it can devalue a model. This happened to the Adidas NMD: a hit when it was released in 2015, it was shunned just two years later. The same is true of rereleases. Rereleasing a sneaker more than once makes it less rare and may cause a price to plummet—a frequent occurrence, with manufacturers repeatedly restocking. Lastly, good or bad buzz can also make an impact, and not necessarily the way you might expect: a pair that is surrounded by controversy, even if it threatens a brand's reputation, generally becomes a hot item.

Social media also influences the sneaker stock market. An influencer who posts pictures wearing a particular model, like Kylie Jenner in her SB Dunks, can cause its price to skyrocket, whether or not it's a limited edition or a new release. And fashion dictates that designs can quickly become popular or obsolete, such as the most imposing of chunky sneakers, Balenciaga's Triple S. Similarly, when a colorway is popular, related searches immediately increase, and the value of those products soars. So price variations on the resale market are of constant concern. And size matters: the same model may be priced differently because the smallest and largest sizes are generally manufactured in fewer quantities and are therefore likely to sell for higher prices. It's the same old story— Economics 101.

As with any market, real-life events have a direct influence on resale values. While the economic context and inflation have been identified as causes for the significant drop in prices in 2022, another more indicative example is the tragic death of Virgil Abloh in November 2021, which triggered an immediate resurgence in interest in his creations. Sales of Off-White sneakers increased drastically the day he died, causing the shoes to soar in value. The iconic Air Jordan 1 High Chicago from Abloh's The Ten collection doubled in price, from $5,000 to $10,000, in a matter of hours.

Guess What ?

Facing page
The Ten pack from the OffWhite × Nike collaboration. Designer Virgil Abloh's incredible success continued on the resale market, triggering dizzying prices.

Right, top and bottom
Resale platforms always manage to get their hands on large stocks for highly anticipated releases, as illustrated here with pairs of Nike × Sacai and Yeezy Slides.

This is the dark side of success. Counterfeiting developed in response to a strong demand for sneakers that outstrips supply. The phenomenon emerged in the boom years of the 1980s, when enthusiasm began to grow and when brands relocated production to China. This outsourcing led to

Counter

In addition to a lucrative resale market, sneaker hype is driving a thriving counterfeit industry. It's the bane of brands, who have difficulty controlling the problem, and retailers, who are doing everything they can to combat it. Here's how fakes have wormed their way into the business.

domestic manufacturing expertise, and China became the epicenter of counterfeit production. Much like the resale market, fakes kept pace with evolutions in sneaker culture, but to an even greater degree. The latest major report from the OECD indicates that shoes were the most copied items in 2016, in a market worth nearly $500 billion annually. And the spread of fakes has only intensified in the intervening years.

Counterfeits range from crude reproductions to perfect replicas—sometimes better made than the originals, according to experts—as counterfeiters work to satisfy clients who are

more or less demanding. The most meticulous counterfeiters ideally obtain the sneaker before its release. That's where the geographic proximity of brand suppliers comes into play: counterfeiters bribe factory employees, both to glean information about future productions and to obtain a sample—a

disappear and reappear under other names. Lawsuits result in judgments by default, as in the case of Nike's 2013 suit against six hundred Chinese counterfeiters, who were ordered to pay $1.8 billion in damages—but they could never be made to settle up, because they couldn't be identified.

feits:
The Flip Side of
Fame

prototype made before the finished product—that they then study in order to make the best copy possible. Similarly, they will seek out material suppliers, other suppliers often located onsite, before undertaking a painstaking assembly process, often using the same machines as legitimate sneaker suppliers. In some cases, the reproduction can hit the market up to three months before the original.

When the time comes to market their products online or via social media, counterfeiters might try to fool consumers by advertising authentic sneakers, or else take the opposite approach and make it clear they're selling fakes—an up-front strategy that stems from the fact that 60 percent of counterfeit purchases are now voluntary. That's the price of fame for sportswear brands, whose focus on limited editions has pushed some clients toward fakes rather than the high-priced goods on the resale market. They're fighting the problem, but not to much effect. They report retailers who sell fakes, but these almost all

The war is therefore being fought on other fronts. It was once again up to Nike, who successfully pushed a bill through Congress giving United States customs agents more latitude to intercept counterfeits, and even provided them with a tool to help authenticate sneakers. Indeed, authentication is a central concern of the resale market, which relies on the promise of certified products. So resale platforms have adopted the same approach as brands: each sneaker sold passes through their warehouses, where experts examine them from every angle, and the transaction is validated only after the shoes have been deemed authentic. It is humans who do the authenticating, which means that some copies might slip through, but employees are regularly trained to prevent these errors— some even buy counterfeits for this very purpose. They are obliged to, since the phenomenon is not about to let up. One thing is certain: as long as sneakers have value, counterfeits won't be far behind.

Facing page, left
As soon as the platform receives a pair of sneakers, employees begin authenticating them. A certificate of authentication is slipped into each box.

Facing page, right
A common scene during legit checks: odor is one of the key elements used to verify a sneaker's authenticity.

How to Authe a Sneaker

Seams and Materials

The devil is in the detail. Once you have a pair in hand, you have to examine it for the slightest anomaly. While traces of glue are not a dealbreaker, the regularity of the seams, the quality of the materials, and the shape of the inserts must be flawless. Experts use blue light to inspect manufacturing elements.

Packaging

The authentication process starts with the packaging. Each brand has boxes with unique details, where information is printed in precise locations. The box and the tissue paper are the first elements to be analyzed.

nticate

Smell
Sneakers have specific odors. Authenticators are often compared to the "noses" working in the perfume industry, because of their keen sense of smell, which can instantly identify a product's origins—an expertise born of experience.

Tags
These details are often neglected by counterfeiters. The labels on the box as well as inside a sneaker can be revealing. An incorrectly applied tag, a missing size, or a convoluted QR code are red flags.

Guess What? "I love counterfeits.... It's better than a great review in *Vogue*. If it's working to the point at which other people can profit, that means it's really working. You're not taking anything away from me, you're actually advertising more," said Virgil Abloh, in February 2017, as he summed up the thinking commonly attributed to brands— that counterfeiting should be viewed in a positive light, as it is the ultimate indicator of desirability. But the designer changed his mind several months later, after his collection with Nike, The Ten, was released, and he registered a number of complaints against sites that he accused of selling fakes. This time, he argued that counterfeits were harming the chances for his brand Off-White to attract new customers. Faced with a fake... it's complicated!

The Most Expens Sneakers

1 Air Jordan 13

$2.2 million

The all-time record was beaten on April 11, 2023, at Sotheby's auction house. The most expensive sneaker in history is now the Air Jordan 13 Bred worn by Michael Jordan during game two of the 1998 NBA final against the Utah Jazz—the last game played and won by the legendary player, who announced his second retirement from basketball when the series ended.

2 Nike Air Yeezy 1

$1.8 million

For two years, the most expensive sneaker was a prototype of the Nike Air Yeezy 1, worn ahead of release by Kanye West at the 2008 Grammy Awards ceremony. It was sold at auction at Sotheby's in April 2021, tripling the previous record.

ive
of All Time

Some sneakers achieve astronomical prices. However, record-making sneaker prices generally fall outside the traditional resale market, and often concern pairs that have been worn during legendary moments in history—most of them starring Michael Jordan.

3
Nike Air Ship
$1.47 million

This pair, worn by Michael Jordan on November 1, 1984, and signed by the man himself, was the very first Nike sneaker he wore. Before receiving his signature model, he chose to play in Air Ship sneakers.

4
Air Jordan 1 High
$615,000

MJ wore this pair on August 25, 1985, during a friendly game in Trieste, Italy, that was made memorable when the player shattered the backboard doing a slam dunk. The pair broke the record for the most expensive sneakers in history in August 2020, at an auction at Christie's.

5
Air Jordan 1 High
$560,000

Another pair worn by His Airness, also a 1985 Air Jordan 1 High in the iconic white, red, and black colorway. It tripled its estimated value to sell for over half a million dollars at Sotheby's in May 2020.

6
Nike Waffle Racing Flat "Moon Shoe"

$437,500

The "Moon Shoe" was one of the first shoes manufactured by Nike, for the 1972 Olympic Games. This pair was one of only twelve ever produced, and the only one that had not been worn.

8
Nike Mag "Back to the Future"

$200,000

The Nike Mag is a legendary sneaker designed by Tinker Hatfield for the movie *Back to the Future Part II*, released in 1989. Nike produced two limited-edition runs, in 2011 and 2016. The most recent version was equipped with LEDs and an automatic lacing system, just like in the movie. One copy sold at a charity auction for $200,000.

9
Converse Fastbreak

$190,373

Before signing a partnership with Nike, Michael Jordan regularly wore Converse sneakers. This might even be the last pair he wore, sighted during the gold medal game at the 1984 Olympics.

7
Louis Vuitton × Nike Air Force 1 Low

$352,800

Virgil Abloh's last collab for Louis Vuitton was an Air Force 1. The two hundred pairs produced were sold at auction after his death to benefit his foundation. They brought in over $23 million in total—the first lot alone sold for $352,800.

10
Air Jordan 11 "Space Jam"

$176,400

These unique Air Jordan 11s were designed specifically for Michael Jordan to wear in the 1996 movie *Space Jam*. He didn't end up wearing them, but one collector thought they were still worth a fortune.

Bonus
Nike Mag "Back to the Future II"

$92,100

This sale would likely have made the top ten most expensive pairs in history— if it hadn't been for a missing shoe. The original 1989 Mag, created for *Back to the Future Part II*, was sold on eBay for nearly $100,000, despite a missing right sneaker and extensive damage.

Above
Michael J. Fox as Marty McFly in *Back to the Future Part II*, wearing the famous Nike Mags.

"Resale
hasn't peaked yet—
far fr

Kilian Dris,
founder of Kikikickz

Kilian Dris has been a sneaker collector since he was a kid. He founded Kikikickz: a resale website specializing in rare and limited-edition sneakers. We met with him at the height of the company's success.

How did you come to be a sneaker reseller?

I was attracted to sneakers from a very young age and started collecting when I was twelve. My obsession grew with each campout, as I made new friends, and when I discovered sneaker culture. Soon resale became the logical next step to expand my collection. I think that all resellers follow the same path: you buy a pair and then sell it to buy others, so you don't have to rely on your allowance all the time. Later on, I met my current partners, and this encouraged me to launch Kikikickz.

"Sneakers are hot now, but there's still room for growth."

How do you explain the fact that this market, initially described as parallel and therefore somewhat opaque, has opened up to the point that it now includes actual companies like Kikikickz?

It's due to two effects. On the one hand, sneakers have gone mainstream: most people wear them now, even in traditionally formal work environments. On the other, sportswear manufacturers follow a strategy of repeatedly releasing limited-edition products, which generates expectations as well as frustration. Resale is a response to all of that, and that's also what makes it a legitimate market.

The average Joe doesn't necessarily understand how someone could invest large sums of money in a pair of sneakers. How would you justify this phenomenon? How would you explain it?

Sneaker resale is rooted in a concept as old as commerce—the law of supply and demand! The sneaker is hype, anticipation is strong, but there aren't enough pairs to go around. But this isn't what we focus on at Kikikickz. We emphasize the cultural value of a sneaker, its history and codes. Our goal is to democratize and popularize. Sneakers are hot now, but there's still room for growth.

Does the resale market have a long-term future?

Kikikickz was founded in 2020 in a very competitive market, but one that hasn't stopped growing: a sign that resale hasn't peaked yet—far from it. Sneakers have become a part of everyday life, but their value as fashion accessories and collectors' items still isn't obvious for everyone. So this means they have room to gain even more ground, along with the resale market.

om it."

The Fu

Snea

ture of
kers

of

How far will this obsession with sneakers go? Is it just a fashion trend and speculative bubble, or is it a long-term phenomenon and a viable economy? When contemplating the outlook for sneakers, the future looks bright: all forecasts predict that the industry will continue to grow, retail and resale markets alike. The lure of the sneaker is as strong as ever and the business still has plenty of surprises in store, but it will have to adapt to meet today's challenges.

The sneaker craze is far from over. The industry forecast is good, and suggests that sneakers will continue their march into the mainstream, attracting new converts to the sneakerverse on their way.

The sneaker's best days lie ahead: that's the takeaway from predictions shared by sector leaders and financial experts, who are counting on the industry's continued exponential growth, on both the primary and secondary markets. The sneaker industry, which in 2021 was worth more than $100 billion annually, is expected to reach $165 billion in 2030, while the resale market is projected to reach $10 to 30 billion over the same period.

These numbers reveal that the sneaker is more than just a passing trend—it is a long-term phenomenon that continues to attract new fans. No longer viewed as inappropriate attire, even in traditionally formal professional settings, these shoes appeal to more and more people around the world. And although they are no longer as commonplace on the avant-garde scene embodied by Fashion Week runways, where sneakers are being passed over for more classic or trendy shoes, like slip-ons, they still have ample room for growth, both as a fashion accessory and a collectible.

Sne Unlimited Growth?

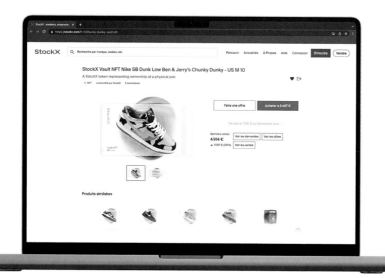

Left
In 2022, the reference resale platform StockX began selling NFTs representing Nike sneakers, drawing the brand's ire.

Facing page
Actor Noah Schnapp, best known for his role in *Stranger Things*, posing with the Rude Kidz NFT created in his likeness. Non-fungible tokens are a new area of growth for the sneaker market.

These projections tend to reinforce brand strategies focused on limited editions, hype, and sold-out models. Rereleases and reinterpretations of retro models will likely take precedence over new products, although environmental responsibility and 3D printing will also play a key role. We can expect to see more collabs and more releases in response to increasing demand.

New possibilities could emerge through the Web 3.0—a new iteration of the Internet that includes blockchain and NFT technology,

other new participants are entering the market, and will continue to do so.

On top of that, the evolution of the sneaker game surely has some surprises in store, given Nike's now regular attacks on various stakeholders and the persistent rumor that the brand will eventually cut ties with retailers to sell its products through its own channels, which raises questions about the subsequent accessibility of sneakers. The future is certainly bright, but it remains to be defined.

akers:

and the metaverse—which all market players are investing in. In any case, no one doubts they will be successful. It remains to be seen if this success will trickle down to the resale market, as usual.

The current tension on the secondary market, caused by the economic context and the decisions of the sportswear giants, could easily lead to a pessimistic outlook. But the fact remains that the resale market is still in its infancy. Certain regions have yet to fully enter it: China, for instance, where interest in sneakers is still new, and which is expected to galvanize the industry in the next few years. So, although some players are disappearing,

Is the boundary between retail and resale likely to become more porous, as past collaborations between StockX and manufacturers suggest? It doesn't appear so. The amicable association between Nike and StockX ended in 2022 when the Swoosh filed a lawsuit against the platform for marketing NFTs representing the brand's sneakers—and for selling counterfeits. Is the Swoosh showing signs of envy for resale's share of industry spoils? It certainly seems that way, given its intensified battle against bots and its related initiatives, such as restocking and selling used pairs. Watch this space!

Innovation
and

The crest of the sneaker wave is still on the horizon, and it may bring surprises with it. In the wake of rereleases, brands continue to innovate to respond to the future needs of consumers, and new technologies already in use could very well shake up the industry.

Sneakers are no longer simply sports equipment, but they remain vehicles for innovation. Brands are still driven to make the best sneaker; behind reinterpretations of retro models, they continuously develop new technology to anticipate needs for sports and everyday use. Whether it's improving cushioning, optimizing the manufacturing process, or offering stronger or more sustainable materials, sportswear manufacturers continue to compete with each other.

Nike and Adidas have been prolific innovators in the last decade. The Swoosh unveiled the stretchy, one-piece Flyknit upper; the ZoomX Vaporfly Next%, an ultra-performance runner with a carbon-fiber plate; the self-adjusting "adaptive fit" HyperAdapt; and the first hands-free sneaker, Go FlyEase. Adidas impressed consumers with Primeknit, the Boost sole, and 3D printing, which it was the first to incorporate on a large scale. This technology, which all sportswear manufacturers are now developing with the help of specialized companies, could very well revolutionize the industry.

Above
3D technology gives designers free rein over their creativity, opening new fields of possibility.

Facing page
The 3D-printed Heron01 sneaker, created by designer Heron Preston, is made without seams or glue, and is entirely recyclable.

158

With 3D printing, known as additive manufacturing, objects can be created using three-dimensional modeling. Based on a computer design, a software "slicing" program uses technical specifications to translate the drawing into a language the printer understands; the printer then applies the material in layers to create the component. Used in many fields, the technology has gained prominence in the sneaker industry in recent years, moving from prototyping into mass production, and from printing individual components to producing entire models, such as the Heron01 by designer Heron Preston. This particular market is expected to generate $8 billion in 2030, following annual increases of 20 percent.

Beyond the figures, 3D printing has incredible potential: it can be used to create custom, personalized sneakers based on a smartphone scan of a customer's feet. In addition to automation and flexibility in design, it favors fast manufacturing that reduces waste, encourages the use of organic or recycled material, and facilitates recycling at the end of the product's life cycle. While it doesn't appear ready to compete with assembly lines, additive manufacturing consolidates solutions to today's major challenges, and allows us to envision a future that meets expectations of customization and environmental responsibility. Promising indeed.

Revolution
Afoot

Guess What ?

3D printing has many qualities, and its use has encouraged sportswear manufacturers to consider bringing production home. Adidas made an attempt in 2017 when it opened two Speed-factories for additive manufacturing: one in Germany and one in the United States. But the Three Stripes closed both sites three years later, once again outsourcing production to Asia.

Officially, the company stated it was "for better utilization of production capacity and more flexibility in product design," but media reports have suggested that automation proved more costly than anticipated, while the German manufacturer had expected drastic cost reductions. 3D printing promises to be advantageous, but we've yet to make the most of its full potential.

There is nothing new about customizing sneakers—it has always been popular. But as the market continues to grow, customization is showing great promise as a new sector.

Customization is at the heart of sneaker culture. When the hip-hop world adopted sneakers in the 1980s, members personalized their kicks with laces and paint to finesse their outfits and set themselves apart from the crowd. The wish for a unique sneaker that expresses their personality and style has continued to inspire sneaker fans. As always, brands have successfully harnessed this desire.

Although Vans allowed its customers to customize their sneakers before hip-hop had even been invented, Nike explored the concept in more depth through its iD program launched in 1999. The initially limited, appointment-based service gave customers the chance to create their own version of a sneaker and was an immediate success. Now called By You, the program is accessible to anyone via Nike's website. Meanwhile, the company developed an exclusive program, Bespoke, that lets shoppers choose from among four hundred colors and materials to create a custom sneaker with the help of a designer.

Today, every brand has a customization service to respond to growing demand. You only have to look at the number of articles

Customiza
Timeless
Tomorrow's

singing the praises of DIY or check out the interest in custom designs on social media to get an idea of how popular customization is. Some specialists, such as The Shoe Surgeon, have even collaborated with leaders in the field, but brands remain wary of large-scale marketing campaigns that use their trademarks. Nike, for example, has filed multiple suits against customizers in recent years—a sign that brands intend to keep a tight rein on the business potential of customization.

Sneakers are expected to attract even more fans, so the desire to stand out, to have a pair unlike any other, will be increasingly pervasive. Services are therefore likely to take the form of exclusive models, like Nike Bespoke, to support an overall strategy

based on limited editions and to evolve toward new innovations. 3D printing technology, which is rapidly expanding, is the ideal response to this trend and promises to meet every expectation in terms of morphology and design. Creating the sneaker of your dreams in-store using 3D printers is one future possibility that is widely discussed in sneaker media. One thing is sure: tomorrow's services and products will align with consumers more than ever.

tion:
Tradition, Trend

Facing page
Customization is at the core of sneaker culture and is still gaining ground, reflecting a growing desire to stand out.

Below
Many sneaker fans try their hand at customization, buying entirely white models and then applying colors to them.

Guess What ? The last custom sneaker to make an impression was the work of rapper Lil Nas X. The artist asked the street-art collective MSCHF to make a custom, devil-themed Air Max 97. Featuring details like a black and red colorway, a drop of human blood in the air bubble, a pentagram pendant attached to the laces—and a production run of 666—the Satan Shoes caused outrage in the United States. Nike was quick to respond, asserting that the model had been produced without the company's authorization, and filed a lawsuit for counterfeit and trademark infringement. The dispute was eventually settled out of court, and the Satan Shoes were withdrawn from sale.

Growing concerns about the environment have influenced consumer trends, including on the sneaker market. Sportswear manufacturers have launched a slew of eco-friendly lines and initiatives, while many new brands have been founded on promises of sustainability. All praiseworthy, but do they really go far enough?

Environmental responsibility is no longer just a promise to be ethical; it has become a business imperative for many brands. Consumers, who are now well aware of environmental issues, are driving this shift. And according to a number of studies, they place great importance on sustainability when choosing to make a purchase. Sneakers are no exception, especially since they are part of the fashion industry, which is known to be one of the most polluting on the planet. In recent years, large manufacturers have begun grappling with the issue and now offer an increasing number of "eco-friendly" sneakers.

Eco

RECYCLING +
DONATION

NE JETEZ PAS, DONNEZ!
NOUS NETTOYONS ET
DONNONS OU RECYCLONS
VOS ANCIENNES AFFAIRES
POUR LEUR DONNER UNE
SECONDE VIE UNE FOIS
QUE VOUS N'EN AVEZ
PLUS BESOIN.

RECYCLING +
DONATION

Nike, which launched the "Reuse-a-shoe" initiative in 1993 to tackle the challenge of recycling sneakers, has embarked on a zero-waste, carbon-neutral strategy called "Move to Zero." Its pinwheel logo encompasses several products made with a percentage of recycled materials: Space Hippie, Flyleather, Crater, and Next Nature. A vegan line called Better is said to be in the works. Adidas has gone even further: in 2015, the company signed a partnership with the NGO Parley for the Oceans, which led to the development of models in a polyester material called Primeblue made from recycled plastic waste that was salvaged from beaches and coastal areas to avoid polluting the ocean. The three-stripe brand, which has committed to using only recycled plastic in its products by 2024, has also developed the Clean Classic line, which makes use of Primegreen, another eco-friendly fabric. The brand most

Facing page
The Sean Wotherspoon × Adidas Superstar. Very involved with the environmental movement, the American designer has made it a point of honor to use only sustainable materials in his footwear collaborations.

Above
A Nike bin labeled "Move to Zero," where customers can leave products that they no longer use, so they can be repurposed.

recently made waves when it released a Stan Smith Mylo made of a mushroom-based leather substitute.

In addition to recycled materials, plant-based matter is widely used to make sneakers, especially by companies with environmentally responsible aims. The French brand Veja is a pioneer in the field, and this promising sector has given rise to many footwear brands in recent years. They're the ones driving new consumer habits, and it's no longer unusual to see uppers made from grape, corn, or cactus leather, seaweed soles, or cork insoles. The range of materials is impressive. But while green sneakers may be all the rage, doubts remain. What about recycling at the end of the product's life cycle? There's no clear feedback on the subject and for good reason: sneakers are hard to recycle. They contain an average of fifteen different materials, each with a specific recycling stream, which makes the process tricky— when the presence of glue doesn't make it altogether impossible.

In 2019, Adidas unveiled the FutureCraft Loop, a 100-percent recyclable sneaker. According to the brand, consumers can return the shoe at the end of its life cycle, and the constituent materials will be used over and over again to make new shoes. The brand expanded the project with an entire line known as Made To Be Remade, and

logy:
A Whole New Game

WHY I RUN FOR THE OCEANS... HOW WE CAN

cultivates a marketing strategy based on the argument that financial objectives and the protection of the planet are not mutually exclusive. But these efforts are often confronted with another obstacle in the endeavor to reduce the environmental impact of sneakers: production. Adidas, like all major manufacturers, outsources production to Asia. There is more to creating eco-friendly sneakers than the use of recycled and recyclable materials; they should be locally made with local materials to support local business, and depend on environmentally respectful processes. In other words, genuine eco-friendly sneakers are not all that common, and the term often smacks of greenwashing.

Above
Adidas has positioned itself in the eco-friendly sneaker niche through a partnership with the non-profit Parley for the Oceans, which provides the brand with plastic salvaged from the oceans.

Facing page
Nike Dunk Low Next Nature "White Mint" and "Pale Coral." The brand from Beaverton, Oregon, now releases many of its classics in versions made from recycled materials.

In 2019, 24.3 billion shoes, sneakers included, were produced, releasing more than seven hundred million tons of CO_2—an output equivalent to that of a country like Germany. Production is largely carried out in Asia where highly polluting coal is essential to the industry, as is the case in China, the world's largest manufacturing economy. Geographical distance also means planet-harming transport: a sneaker may travel over ten thousand miles (16,000 km) by boat before landing on the shelves. Nike and Adidas are working on these issues, and insist that they intend to reduce their carbon footprints by 30 percent by 2030. We'll check in for an update.

Toward a
More Incl

Inclusivity, like environmental responsibility, is a major preoccupation today. Sportswear brands have tackled this issue as well, in marketing campaigns and products. But there's still some way to go.

Today, sneakers transcend the generations and specific identities, and manufacturers now seek to capitalize on this. Nike, Adidas, Reebok, and Puma have all recently unveiled campaigns celebrating individuality, diversity, or body positivity, and voice their support for LGBTQIA+ issues and gender equality. These praiseworthy initiatives disguise the fact that such efforts have been late in coming: the first women's sneaker, the Reebok Freestyle, didn't come out until 1982, and a woman athlete wasn't given a signature model until 1995.

The sneaker industry has never had much of a reputation for gender equality. In the past, women who were keen to acquire a pair of these shoes, which had long—and somewhat curiously—been associated with men, were faced with stereotypical, preconceived ideas and messaging that suggested wearing sneakers might be unfeminine or inelegant. It is only in the last few decades that the barriers have fallen, sneakers are more popular than ever, and women have embraced the trend once and for all—a reflection of societal changes, a demand for equality, and a show of empowerment.

Brands have taken note and expanded their meager offerings by releasing more and more sneakers for women, including collaborations with figures like Rihanna and Beyoncé, with a "for us, by us" marketing vibe. But this is not to say that the needs of consumers are being heard and met. In an interview with French online media company Konbini, Aleali May—a style blogger, model, and influencer who regularly collaborates with Jordan Brand—summed up the criticism featured on social networks and certain specialized media outlets of sneakers marketed at women: "When people use the words 'girls' and 'streetwear' together, I feel like they're projecting the image of one single type of woman. Which is a mistake, because there are an infinite number of girls with an infinite number of styles in the streetwear scene."

When collaborations driven by women are incorporated into a limiting, gendered framework, feminine exclusives usually boil down to very "girly" design elements—glitter and sequins, rhinestones and jewels, pink colorways, and platform soles. May strives to overcome this by demonstrating that women are more than capable of creating shoes that are equally coveted by men, and she does this brilliantly, like her counterparts Yoon Ahn of Ambush and Chitose Abe of Sacai. These inspiring success stories could make a case for the end of market segmentation, but it will be a while before

the sneaker game is genderless: women are often excluded from purchasing specific pairs, especially the most hyped collaborations, because their sizes aren't available. There's a long road ahead.

Guess What? According to a report provided by online platform StockX on its first five years in operation, resale volumes of women's shoes increased by a factor of 1,500 between 2016 and 2021. In concrete terms, the same number of women's sneakers were purchased every four hours in 2021 as in the entire year 2016.

usive
Market
(At Last!)

The Limi

of Commitment

Sportswear manufacturers continue to proclaim their commitment to major causes, from sustainability to inclusivity. But do they really want to change things? Nothing could be less certain.

In 1996, the image of a Pakistani child sewing a Nike soccer ball was seen around the world. It was the culmination of a series of scandals involving major sports equipment manufacturers, adding to an already long list of accusations about working conditions at their suppliers' factories. Nearly three decades later, the problems remain, despite audits, a desire for transparency, and gestures toward sustainability initiatives. Controversies regularly tarnish the image of the main footwear makers—evidence that unethical practices continue. Today, just as in the past, these companies only change their behavior when faced with increased public pressure.

The reality of the exploitation of oppressed peoples, such as the Uyghurs, cut through the rhetoric in 2021, and marketing campaigns advocating equality and diversity were revealed to be little more than smoke screens. As proof of their cynicism, the major sports equipment manufacturers are gradually leaving China, where they relocated their production in the 1980s, in favor of countries like Indonesia and Vietnam: salaries have risen in China, so sportswear giants have set their sights on other countries to preserve their impressive margins. Nothing can counter the insatiable desire for profit. Not even the environmental crisis.

After questioning the ecological value of a product assembled on the other side of the world by a polluting industry, it is tempting to see promises of sustainability as simply a response to new consumer expectations, rather than as a genuine desire to change

the world; to see it as self-serving marketing, or even greenwashing, when a brand oversells its commitment while continuing with its usual drops. A simple look at the release calendar is evidence enough: the sector's leaders have cranked out eco-friendly sneakers in recent seasons, not to replace a portion of the preexisting offer, but to add to it. The benefits for the planet are cancelled out by the burden of overproduction. A commitment to sustainability should mean producing fewer and better quality products, but new releases roll out at a frantic pace, which even the Covid-19 pandemic couldn't slow, despite promises from many decision makers in the fashion industry. The world hasn't changed, and the mix of hype, releases, and sold-out strategies is alive and well. Products are promoted on social media, that vehicle of rapid obsolescence, where desire evaporates as quickly as it appears. Sustainability should also mean encouraging people to buy less.

But are brands always evil manipulators and customers their innocent victims? The reality is not so black-and-white. Although studies indicate that consumers are more concerned than ever about environmental issues, sneaker purchases have never been higher. The fact that sneakers are objects of obsession, subject to accumulation and collection, does nothing to mitigate the contradiction. Many sneakerheads admit that they resumed their frenzied collecting after reducing, or even stopping, their habit in the wake of a scandal regarding a manufacturer. The ills of overconsumption are no doubt shared—because with information easier to access than ever, no one can feign ignorance.

ts

Sportswear manufacturers—
Nike and Adidas especially—
are often challenged on
social media: users' criticism
focuses on brands' claims
to support causes.

#Nike doesn't do it to reduce its
waste. They don't care about the
environment. As consumers buy
more and more second-hand stuff,
#Nike is trying to make money on
this market. We see them

07:08 · 13/04/2021 · Twitter

2 J'aime

Nike has clearly refused
to end the slavery of Uighur
Muslims. SHAME.

15:19 · 09/07/2020 · Twitter for Android

cité 74 J'aime

Nike: literally have Uighur blood
on their hands.

Also Nike : Making a complaint for
a drop of human blood

13:39 · 30/03/2021 · Twitter for iPhone

26 Retweets 141 J'aime

Raphael Glucksmann ✔
@rglucks1

@Nike we play
#BlackLivesMatters humanists
and exploit Uighur slaves? Isn't
there some kind of contradiction
here? It's up to you
to put an end to this shame.
Just do it.

20:09 · 29/06/2020 · Twitter for iPhone

329 Retweets 25 Tweets cités 599 J'aime

Must boycott Nike, they exploit
Uighur slaves!!!

02:38 · 10/07/2020 · Twitter for Android

Good mentality @Nike and
@adidasFR. They refuse to allow
their items to be donated or resold
second hand. So they are left in
a trashcan with boxcutter strokes.
#Ecology, human, words well
forgotten by your companies!
#shame

14:21 · 02/11/2019 · Twitter for iPhone

1 Retweet

@Nike and ecology make 2 ! A big
box for a little thing that fits in a small
bag

12:41 · 05/06/20

#ABrandAQuote you wear Nike
on your feet while the Uighurs
wear chains on their feet

21:13 · 13/11/2020 · Twitter for Android

3 J'aime

Guess What ?

"What drives me is not money. I'm not in this for money anymore. What I want to do before I go to that great shoe factory in the sky, is make this as good a company as I can. I have a basic belief, having been burned on it once, that Americans do not want to make shoes," explained Nike founder Phil Knight to director Michael Moore in his 1997 documentary *The Big One*. At the time, the Swoosh was in turmoil over its choice to outsource to Indonesia, where it employed children with the support of a repressive military regime. Moore got Knight to promise that if he could find volunteers in a city in Michigan, the CEO would consider opening a factory there. Despite videos proving local support for the idea, Knight ultimately refused. "I think that any unemployed person will say that they would like any job, but that given a choice, Americans really don't want to work in shoe factories. I still believe that." And apparently he still does.

"Maybe we'll start settling for new sneakers for our avatars in Web 3.0, **rather than**

Sarah Andelman, cofounder of Colette

Director of the creative consulting agency Just an Idea, Sarah Andelman was the cofounder, artistic director, and buyer for the Paris concept store Colette. A global fashion mecca during its twenty-year run, from 1997 to 2017, the boutique also contributed to the influence of sneakers through ultra-limited collabs. Here, Andelman gives us her perspective on the industry.

You were instrumental in the sneaker's transformation from sports gear to fashion accessory. How did this happen, in your opinion?
For me, sneakers have always been an everyday fashion accessory. They have been cult objects since the 1980s, but it's true, I witnessed their arrival in luxury brand collections. And so I saw a growing number of people include sneakers in their look the same way they would the latest pair of heels.

"For me, sneakers have always been an everyday fashion accessory."

What does this transition tell us about fashion and society more broadly? Basically, how do you explain the boom in sneakers?
Practically speaking, I would say that it is undeniably a question of comfort. We live in a world where everything goes very quickly, you have to be fast. And we might be reaching a form of standardization as streetwear permeates fashion collections.

The sneaker industry has changed a lot since the early days of Colette. How do you view the market now?
We may have reached saturation. During the years that Colette was open, every brand increased drops. I think that consumers are getting tired and prefer to concentrate on what really interests them, hence a more segmented offer, with pairs specifically for skateboarding, basketball, hiking, etc. Sneakers are universal, but influences differ. I also hope that brands will seriously consider notions like sustainable development.

Brands have indeed tackled major current concerns like the environmental crisis and inclusivity through products and marketing campaigns. But are their efforts sufficient and genuine? After all, don't these commitments run counter to their sales strategies?
I agree, things really need to slow down. There needs to be real awareness and proof of it. I think that the younger generations are very concerned and could force a paradigm shift.

How do you envision the sneaker's long-term future? With ongoing innovations like 3D printing, isn't the future in the hands of consumers? Will the frustration generated by the current system give way to personalized, on-demand services?
I think there will always be a respect for designers and design studios; not everyone has that talent. On the other hand, maybe we'll start settling for new sneakers for our avatars in Web 3.0, rather than in real life.

in real life."

This
Obsession
with
Sneak

ers!

"Put on your sneakers!" The origins of the sports shoe is summed up in this familiar command uttered by generations of parents to their children: these shoes were, quite simply, for playing sports in.

They still fulfill this role, of course, but on the street sneakers have surpassed their primary function: they have become markers of message, style, and personality.

We love them, whether they're minimalist or multicolored, with three stripes or a Swoosh, conceived by a famous designer or from a cult streetwear brand—basically, we love them all. Sneakers unite, transcending age, gender, social background, culture, and sartorial style.

They are seen as a social phenomenon—a vehicle for obsession and desire, for speculation and profit. But, above all, sneakers are cultural objects; from college campuses to urban streets to the runways of Fashion Week, and from underground protest movements to the mainstream, sneakers tell our story.

The humble sports shoe has become a symbol of our era. It has come a long way, but we'd venture to say that the finish line is not yet in sight, and that the sneaker will remain a testament to the long road traveled.

Sneakers: what an obsession!

Photographic Credits

14
© Granger/
Bridgeman Images

15
© Bridgeman
Images

16
© Photopress
Archiv/
Keystone/
Bridgeman Images

17 (top)
© Education
Images/
Universal Images
Group/
Getty Images

17 (bottom)
© Roger-Viollet

18
© R.K.O. PICTURES/
Diltz/
Bridgeman Images

18
© Mirrorpix/
Getty Images

19
© Everett/
Aurimages

20
© Michael Ochs
Archives/
Getty Images

21 (top)
© Beatriz Braga/
Pexels

21 (bottom)
© Joe Sohm/
Visions of America/
Universal Images
Group
via Getty Images

22
© Paul Natkin/
WireImage/
Getty Images

23
© Everett/
Aurimages

24
© PYMCA/Universal
Images Group/
Getty Images

25
© Bridgeman
Images

26
© Anthony Barboza/
Getty Images

27
© Barbara Alper/
Getty Images

28
© Greg White/
Fairfax Media/
Getty Images

29
© Pool Ducasse/
Lounes/Gamma-
Rapho
via Getty Images

32
© Everett/
Aurimages

33
© Jean-Erick
Pasquier/
Gamma-Rapho

36
© Bettmann/
Getty Images

37 (left)
© Nike

37 (right)
© Manuel Mittelpunkt

37 (bottom)
© Bridgeman Images

40
© Nike

41 (top)
© Nike

41 (bottom)
© Nike

46
© The Adidas
Archive

47 (top)
© Everett/
Aurimages

47 (bottom)
© Brauner/Ullstein
Bild/Getty Images

50
© Randy Brooke/
Getty Images/AFP

51 (bottom)
© Rich Fury/VF20/
Getty Images

55
© Nathan Merchadier

56
© Sven Simon/AKG

57 (top)
© NCAA Photos/
Getty Images

57 (bottom)
© The Advertising
Archives/
Bridgeman Images

60
© Yunghi Kim/
The Boston Globe/
Getty Images

61 (top)
© Reebok

61 (bottom)
© Reebok

64
© Stan Grossfeld/
The Boston Globe/
Getty Images

65 (top)
© Nike

65 (bottom)
© The Advertising
Archives/
Bridgeman Images

68
© New Balance

69 (top)
© New Balance

69 (bottom)
© New Balance

73
© Suzanne Daniels

74 (left)
© ASICS

74 (right)
© ASICS

75 (top)
© ASICS

75 (bottom)
© Everett Collection/
Bridgeman Images

78
© Andrea Leopardi/
Unsplash

79 (top)
© Douglas Bagg/
Unsplash

79 (bottom)
© Ron Grover/
MPTV/Bureau233

87
© Agence/
Bestimage

95 (top)
© Nike

96
© Daniele Venturelli/
Getty Images

97
© Theo Wargo/
Getty Images/AFP

102
© Michael N. Todaro/
Getty Images/AFP

106
© Nike

107
© Lester Cohen/
WireImage/
Getty Images

108
© Tiziano Da Silva/
BestImage

109 (top)
© Wiktor
Szymanowicz/
Future Publishing/
Getty Images

109 (bottom)
© Nap Funtelar/
Unsplash

113
© Leslie Dumeix

114 (top)
© Nike

114 (bottom)
© Chesnot/
WireImage/
Getty Images

115
© Nike

117
© Francois Durand/
Getty Images/AFP

118 (top)
© Epic Games

118 (bottom)
© Kevin Mazur/
Getty Images

119 (top)
© Rick Kern/
WireImage/
Getty Images

119 (bottom)
© Jerritt Clark/
Getty Images/AFP

121
© Gotham/
GC Images/
Getty Images

122
© Nike

123 (top)
© Matt Winkelmeyer/
Getty Images/AFP

129
© Kevin Mazur/
Getty Images for
Universal Music
Group

148
© Cindy Ord/
Getty Images

151
© Everett Collection/
Bridgeman Images

164
© Neilson Barnard/
Getty Images/AFP

166
© Justin Sullivan/
Getty Images/AFP

170
© Stephane
Cardinale –
Corbis/Corbis
via Getty Images

The Publisher and Kikikickz would like to thank
the brands, agencies, and photographers
for kindly granting permission to reproduce
the images that appear in this book.
The Publisher and Kikikickz have made every
effort to identify and contact rights holders.
Any errors or omissions are inadvertent
and will be rectified in subsequent printings
upon notification.

Éditions Flammarion

Editorial Partnerships
Henri Julien and
Emmanuelle Rolland

Editor
Virginie Maubourguet,
assisted by **Léo Rougier**

English Edition

Editorial Director
Kate Mascaro

Editor
Helen Adedotun

Translation from the French
Kate Robinson

Copyediting
Lindsay Porter

Typesetting
Claude-Olivier Four

Proofreading
Bethany Wright

Production
Louisa Hanifi and
Marylou Deserson

Color Separation
**Atelier Frédéric Claudel,
Paris**

Printed in Bosnia and
Herzegovina by **GPS**

Text by
Alexandre Pauwels

Art and Editorial Director
Mathis Bouquillion

Editorial Conception
Juliette Figoni

Design
Louis Desmet and
Thomas Ricard

Originally published
in French as
Sneakers Obsession
© Éditions Flammarion, S.A.,
Paris, 2022
© Kikikickz 2022

English-language edition
© Éditions Flammarion, S.A.,
Paris, 2023
© Kikikickz 2023

editions.flammarion.com
@flammarioninternational

24 25 26   5 4 3

ISBN: 978-2-08-029470-8

Legal Deposit: 03/2023